THE LIZARD IN LANDEWEDNACK

A Village Story

The Lizard History Society 1996

THE LIZARD IN THE PARISH OF LANDEWEDNACK

To Helston

ROAD NAMES AND PLACES OF INTEREST

- ① Light House
- ② Lifeboat Station
- ③ Signal Station (Lloyds)
- ④ The Church
- ⑤ The Chapel
- ⑥ The School
- ⑦ The Stone Cross
- ⑧ Wartha Manor
- ⑨ The Square
- ⑩ The Green
- ⑪ Lion's Den
- ⑫ Hot Point
- ⑬ Polbream Cove
- ⑭ Vellan Drang

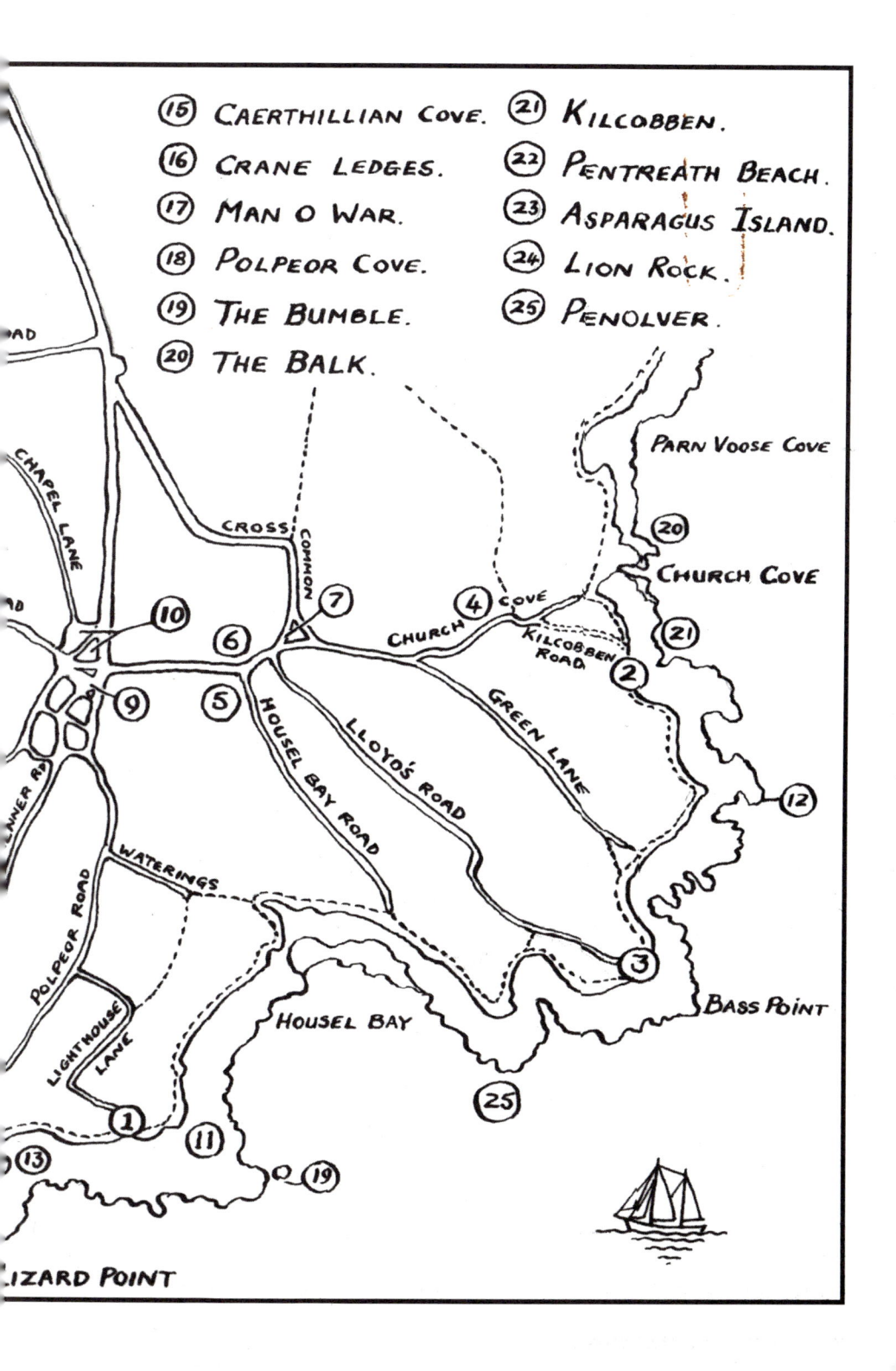

- ⑮ CAERTHILLIAN COVE.
- ⑯ CRANE LEDGES.
- ⑰ MAN O WAR.
- ⑱ POLPEOR COVE.
- ⑲ THE BUMBLE.
- ⑳ THE BALK.
- ㉑ KILCOBBEN.
- ㉒ PENTREATH BEACH.
- ㉓ ASPARAGUS ISLAND.
- ㉔ LION ROCK.
- ㉕ PENOLVER.

First published, with the aid of a grant from the Leader Project *by* The Lizard History Society, Crane Ledges, Man of War View, The Lizard, Cornwall TR12 7NS 1996.
© The Lizard History Society, 1996

No part of this publication may be reproduced, stored in a retrieval system, or transmitted in any form or by any means, electronic or mechanical, photocopying, recording or otherwise without the prior permission of the copyright holder.

Whilst every care has been taken to ensure accuracy, errors may have crept in. Any corrections or additions submitted in writing to The Lizard History Society will be considered for inclusion in future editions of 'The Lizard in Landewednack'.

ISBN 0 9528711 0 6

PRINTED BY
Litho Thermo Printers
Units 13-15 Parc Erissey Ind. Est., New Portreath Road, Redruth, Cornwall TR16 4HW.
Tel: 01209 212200, Fax: 01209 212220.

Copies obtainable from the publishers (price £5.50 to include postage and packing)

CONTENTS

Page 7   Introduction

Page 8   Foundations

Page 28   The Land

Page 68   The Sea

Page 102   Memories & Family Businesses

Page 118   New Horizons

Page 124   Acknowledgements

Introduction

The Lizard. A place of legend, history and mystery. The most southerly peninsula on mainland Britain and ~ the focus of this book ~ its most southerly village.

So much about The Lizard's past is clouded by centuries of isolation. Even today as old generations die away to be replaced by incomers of an ever more mobile society, local knowledge and memories are dying away almost daily. With the pace of change accelerating all the time, the aim of this book is to set down the story of The Lizard village up to the mid-1990s for today's and future residents and visitors.

It covers as many facets of The Lizard as is possible in such a modest publication, from the rocks on which the village is built to the people who have enlivened it. From shipwrecks to smuggling, from the lifeboat to Lloyds Signal Station, from fishing to farming, from serpentine workers to its shops, this is the story of The Lizard, the village at the end of England.

But where to begin? Where better than with the name itself? The parish goes by the lovely lilting title of Landewednack, centred around the centuries-old church and its cove. But it is The Lizard by which most of the world knows the village ~ hence the name of this book, 'The Lizard in Landewednack'.

Why 'The Lizard'? Theories abound, from the scholarly to the everyday. What does seem certain ~ happily given the specific area covered by this book ~ is that the name belonged to the southernmost point before it came to refer to the whole peninsula.

Scholars translate 'Lusart' or 'Lysart', the earliest forms of the name, as meaning High Court or something similar. The Lizard has centuries-old links with West Brittany, and the Breton language of the ninth and tenth centuries is known to have used 'lis' to mean the base for a chief. Perhaps more appealingly for those who love The Lizard scenery, the other main theory comes from the shape of the headland itself. It takes little imagination ~ especially for mariners ~ to see a crouching lizard in the folds of the cliffs. And even today looking from Housel Bay towards Lizard Point, given the right light, the illusion can still be striking.

CHAPTER ONE

Foundations

~ ARCHAEOLOGY AT THE LIZARD ~

Windmill Farm ~
In 1982 George Smith, from the Department of the Environment's Central Excavation Unit, carried out the rescue excavation of a Mesolithic Site at Windmill Farm, Predannack Moor; 1.5 km inland from Kynance Cove. The site, which lies close to a stream bed in the shelter of a dense growth of willows and hazels, was revealed when the field was ploughed for the first time that spring. Further ploughing would have destroyed the ephemeral remains. The excavators uncovered over 4, 000 flint artefacts and 72,000 waste flakes from the site. The preponderance of tools such as scrapers and hammerstones amongst the flint assemblage indicated that the site was probably a fairly long term settlement. The excavated area was thought to represent a central working and cooking zone, with other settlement structures situated beyond this area. Radiocarbon dating from a sample of charcoal-rich soil suggested that the site dates from the fifth millennium BC. Mesolithic flints have been found elsewhere at The Lizard, notably at Polpeor, near Kynance Gate and on top of Asparagus Island at Kynance Cove. Many coastal sites are thought to have been lost because of rises in sea level since the Mesolithic period.

Hervan Menhir ~
This standing stone, perhaps dating from the early Bronze Age (c 2000 BC) lies just off The Lizard ~ Helston road at the entrance to Predannack Airfield. It is set in a garden hedge and very weather worn.

Kynance Gate ~
This ancient settlement at Kynance Gate is located at the edge of an open moorland plateau overlooking Kynance Valley. It is situated in a field named 'Round Close' in the 1840 Tithe Award for Mullion, and is first recorded as 'British Village' on the 1880 Ordnance Survey map. The site's archaeological history begins following a heath fire in 1896, when some members of the Royal Institute of Cornwall spent an afternoon excavating two hutcircles down to 'floor level'.

Apart from visits by curio hunters the site was largely forgotten until the early 1950s, when a schoolboy found some pottery there. This led Ivor Thomas, then headmaster at Lizard School, to initiate a series of excavations which lasted between 1955 and 1964. The site was scheduled in 1956 (Scheduled Monument, Cornwall No. 439) and surveyed by the Ordnance Survey in 1973.

Thomas's excavation demonstrated that the visible structures, two groups of hutcircles, are Iron Age/Romano British (IA/RB) in date and that they overlie extensive remains of Bronze Age activity. The Bronze Age occupation centred on the prominent serpentine outcrop around which the later IA/RB site was built. The remains consisted of clay floors, paving and hearths (including two possible kilns or furnaces) but there were no surviving structures. The finds include large amounts of Trevisker I-III styles of pottery, a considerable quantity of flint and many imported stones and pebbles. Thomas interpreted the site as a Bronze Age workshop where pottery manufacture, metal and stoneworking took place. The finds indicate that occupation of the site occurred between c1400 BC and 1000 BC, when the site was abandoned.

Approximately 750 metres north east of the settlement, on Lizard Downs, is a Bronze Age barrow (burial mound). The barrow is 18 metres in diameter and 1.5 metres high. It is covered with gorse and has evidently been dug into sometime in the past. The barrow probably dates from the Early Bronze Age (c2000 BC to c1500 BC) and would therefore be earlier than the occupation at Kynance Gate. However the mound is a distinct landmark on the featureless moor-land horizon when viewed from the settlement and, similarly, the serpentine outcrop is a landmark when viewed from the barrow. Kynance Gate was reoccupied during the IA/RB period, when the settlement consisted of two contrasting groups of huts. Those to the NNE are freestanding and unenclosed, those to the SSW are set around the serpentine outcrop and linked by walling to form two enclosed areas. The majority of the huts in the SSW group were fully or partly excavated by Thomas, together with large areas inside the enclosure. There were nine circular or oval huts, most with double-faced stone walls infilled with rubble. The three largest are circular and lie to the west of the outcrop. A wall, linking these and another smaller hut on the east, runs around the outcrop forming a small enclosure. The wall continues north east of the entrance, joining the enclosure to three more small stone huts. The NNE group consists of at least five free standing huts, each is approximately 9 metres in diameter with walls averaging 0.4 metres high. Only one of these huts was excavated by Thomas. Today the site is covered by dense gorse.

Finds from this phase of the excavation, now stored in the Helston Museum, include ceramics, spindle whorls and glass beads.

On the cliff tops west of Kynance Cove are the walls of another small hutcircle which is linked to the remains of a field system. The field system consists of low stone and earth banks and lynchets which form terraces descending the cliff slope and extending up to the cliff edge. The exact date of the field system is unknown, but it is likely to be Prehistoric and associated with one of the phases of occupation at Kynance Gate.

The excavations at Kynance Gate were published only as a series of notes in the magazine of The Lizard Field Studies Club. Full

**Reconstructed Urn
(middle Bronze Age food pot)
unearthed at Kynance Gate ~**

publication of this important site is much to be desired, as is a large scale survey of the settlement and the field system.

Carngoon Bank ~
In 1978 Colin Hendy discovered large quantities of pottery during land clearance at Carngoon Bank. A trial excavation by Peter Rose of the Cornwall Committee for Rescue Archaeology (now the Cornwall Archaeological Unit) raised questions about the site that only a large scale excavation could answer.

In the autumn and early winter of 1979 the site was excavated by members of the Central Excavation Unit, the Cornwall Archaeological Society and local volunteers under the direction of Fachtna McAvoy. The investigations revealed a 'multi-phase' archaeological site. There was some Mesolithic activity, a Mid-to-Late Bronze Age chipped stone manufactory and a Middle Iron Age artificial pond with retaining bank. The most extensive occupation was during the Romano-British period, dating from the 1st century AD with the greatest activity during the 3rd and 4th centuries, when the site was used as a saltworks. The features associated with saltworking included a large pond, downslope of the main working area, a circular post-built structure with a perimeter gully or drain, and an area of rough cobbling west of the pond.

Four distinct mounds of briquetage were distinguished by the excavators (briquetage is the name given to fragments of coarse reddish brown pottery from shallow rectangular vessels in which the saltwater was evaporated). The circular structure contained clay-lined pits and rectangular stone containers for the pottery vessels.

The archaeological evidence suggested that the saltworking site was abandoned in the 4th century and reoccupied in the 6th century when the building was temporarily reused. A series of ceramic platters were found, three with stamped ornament, but the only structural features associated with this phase were stakeholes. At the southern end of the site were a series of loam filled gullies which formed a small enclosure pre-dating the present hedge. McAvoy considered that the enclosure may correspond to an enclosure shown on a survey of a farm to the south of Lizard Town, dated 1691.

Rounds/Fortified Areas ~
The field names 'Parc an Castle', 'Castle Minot' and 'Gew Dinas' suggest the possible sites of fortified areas or rounds. Rounds are defended farming settlements of the Iron Age/Romano British period.

Carn Caerthillian ~
Three sherds of pottery were found on the footpath down to Pentreath Beach in 1978. Two sherds were classed as Iron Age Cordon Ware, the third, reddish brown in colour with diagonal slashed decoration was identified as Bronze Age.

On Carn Caerthillian are the remains of a field system consisting of slight lynchets. The date of the field system is unknown, it may be Prehistoric.

Pentreath Beach ~
In 1973 sixteen gold bars were found by Nicholas Casley and Steven Richards in a landslip above Pentreath Beach. The bars were approximately 1.5" long and 0.75" diameter; the specific gravity

of the bars were 15.0 to 15.5 which corresponds to the specific gravity of Iron Age coins of the type Gallo-Belgic A. A court enquiry awarded the bars to the two boys who found them.

Asparagus Island ~
One of the archaeological mysteries of The Lizard is the cropmark visible on the grassy top of Asparagus Island in the right weather conditions. The cropmark is rectangular in plan with a series of rectangular subdivisions forming a gridlike internal pattern. The cropmark is a subject of local knowledge but has not been commented on by any academic authority. The date of the cropmark is unknown. Apparently the occupiers of Jolly Town Farm used to pay rent for Asparagus Island. Jolly Town is an 18th century settlement, established for the benefit of the soapstone workers at Gew Graze. If connected with Jolly Town the cropmark could be of comparatively recent date. *Charles Johns.*

~ LANDEWEDNACK PLAIN AN GWARRY ~

A plain an gwarry or 'playing place' was an amphitheatre with an arena. Its exact purpose is unknown but most probably it was used for games such as wrestling or contests, for meetings, for plays or for other ceremonial religious or secular occasions.

According to the 'History of Cornwall' written by the Rev. Polwhele, Vicar of Manaccan, in the early 1800s: On Lizard Downs there is an amphitheatre about a quarter of a mile from Landewednack church. The enclosing bank 117 feet across, is now low and in a state of decay. The old way to the church passes close by the circle, but the new road runs nearly through the middle of it.

In 1851 the remains of a possible plain an gwarry were recorded a quarter of a mile north west of the church although Charles Henderson, the eminent Cornish historian, wrote in the 1920s that 'no sign of it may now be seen. The site is difficult to find, possibly being near the site of the wayside stone cross. It may have been a circular encampment'.

Research is at present in progress to ascertain the exact site and nature of this ancient amphitheatre. (At Ruan Minor a plain an gwarry has been identified opposite the Cherry Tree Garage). *Derry Dobson*

~ SERPENTINE ~

While most of Cornwall is granite, The Lizard peninsula is composed of metamorphic rock and the likelihood therefore of any radon gas within the parish is very small indeed. Metamorphic rocks are those which have been altered by heat or pressure, and the ones in Landewednack are mostly horneblende schists. These produce the impressive coastal scenery of cliffs, caves and sea-stacks like Bumble Rock in Housel Bay, whilst off the Most Southerly Point can be seen what are probably the oldest rocks on the peninsula, the Man of War reef, perhaps 500 million years old. In the northern part of the parish, though, the schists give way to serpentine, which with its distinctive and beautiful appearance is the most famous and characteristic rock of The Lizard. A large part of the peninsula is made up of a serpentine mass, some 20 miles in area, which forms the plateau-like heathland of Goonhilly and Predannack Downs. Serpentine weathers only slowly.

CHAPTER ONE ~ FOUNDATIONS

When it does, it decomposes into an infertile clay, which is almost impermeable to water. As a result the surface of the Downs is often very water logged and boggy in winter or after a summer rain storm. The serpentine reaches the coast at several places, including Kynance Cove, where it forms spectacular cliffs and where pebble-sized samples can be picked up on the beach.

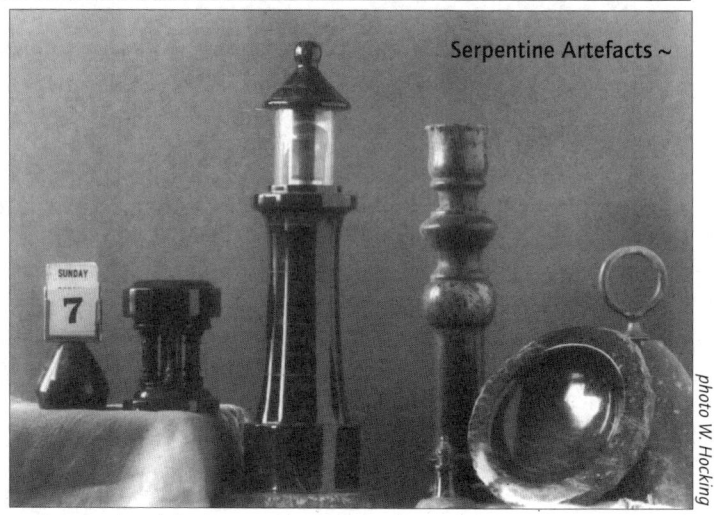

Serpentine Artefacts ~

photo W. Hocking

Serpentine is said to have gained its name from its resemblance to a serpent's skin. In its unpolished state it is rough and unprepossessing but, once polished, its true colours are revealed in bands and veins of red, black, green, grey, white and yellow. The story goes that its potential beauties were first realised when a shipwreck sailor first noticed, standing in the middle of a field, a tall stone, one side of which had been polished by cattle rubbing against it. Others say that it was the use of serpentine blocks as stiles or steps and their subsequent wear by passing feet, which over the years polished the stone and suggested a decorative use for it.

Serpentine is found in three main varieties or forms ~ dunite, tremolite and the one which is most often used to make decorative items, enstatite (or bastite). It has been turned and polished in Landewednack parish (and elsewhere in the peninsula) for, it is said, over 200 years, although no records of turning are known before the early nineteenth century. The stone was certainly being used in its unpolished state as building material four hundred years before that, when the church tower was constructed of alternating blocks of serpentine and granite. The tradition of using unpolished serpentine in the church continued until the middle of the nineteenth century when it was used to replace the damaged pillars of the south doorway and to provide four new pillars for the fifteenth century font. The lectern and pulpit, this time of polished serpentine are also mid-nineteenth century, but as they are large 'monumental items' they would not have been made in the village but have come from the Serpentine Company's works at Poltesco.

In 1828 Mr. Drew whilst working on repairs to The Lizard Lighthouse was said to have been so struck by the beauty of the serpentine stone that he eventually learnt how to manufacture 'useful and beautiful' articles for himself. This suggests that small, ornamental serpentine items were already being made before that date. He appears to have been instrumental in starting a company in Wherrytown in Penzance, where Derbyshire men, expert in making Blue John articles, were employed.

In 1838 the Poltesco Serpentine Works started production, making 'smallish ornaments of one foot high'! For a time during the nineteenth century serpentine goods of all kinds enjoyed great popularity. This was largely due to royal patronage. In 1846 the Royal family were cruising in their yacht when due to seasickness, Prince Albert asked to be put ashore and was landed at

Kynance Cove. There he saw and purchased a serpentine ornament from a certain Thomas and was much impressed by it. He and Queen Victoria having given serpentine their seal of approval, the next few years saw items, both large and small, being installed in royal and noble houses throughout Britain. Elsewhere serpentine enjoyed a success as 'poor man's marble'. In 1848 37 men and a boy were employed in the serpentine trade in Penzance, and over £2,000 worth of serpentine was sent to the Great Exhibition held at the Crystal Palace in 1851, where a prize medal was won.

During the next two decades serpentine continued to gain in popularity and the industry to prosper. In 1835 we learn that a visitor following the cliff path to Mullion found himself in Kynance where there were 'refreshments sold in a little tenement facing the sea, and specimens of serpentine and other rareties'. A few years later in 1863 an advertisement in the West Briton informed 'Excursionists and visitors to Kynance Cove' that William Oliver had 'serpentine ornaments always on sale'.

Kelly's Directory for 1856 mentions that two quarries were in operation at Poltesco. The initials LSC ~ Lizard Serpentine Company ~ are still to be seen today on the gable end of the three-storey warehouse building. In 1873 the Poltesco Marble Company was employing 20 men and three boys, but by about 1893 it had closed. There seem to have been a number of reasons for this. Fickleness of fashion may have had something to do with it; competition from cheap Spanish and Italian marble may also have played a part. Enormous pieces of stone were no longer obtainable, and 'monumental commissions' such as mantel pieces, tables, lecterns, fonts, shop fronts and mammoth pillars like those still to be seen today on the facade of the Bank of England, became an impossibility and, in the light of the recently discovered brittleness of serpentine and its liability to crack under stress, also unwise. The loss at sea of a large uninsured quantity of unfinished articles resulted in a large financial loss for the Company and may well have been the last straw.

Some of the workers thrown out of work by the closure of the Poltesco Factory opened individual serpentine workshops. The cottage industry which resulted, and still continues, at The Lizard, may be said to have originated at Poltesco in the 1890s. One such worker was John Bosustow who had served his apprenticeship at Poltesco. His sons Frank and Charles carried on the tradition and Charles' son Vivian and Frank's son John are both 'turners'. Vivian still has one of the original Poltesco lathes in his workshop in Church Cove.

photo J. Hart

Francis Jose (1836 - 1913) in the doorway of his Serpentine Shop ~

Between the wars there were at one time some 30 small workshops selling a wide variety of beautifully coloured serpentine ornaments to holiday makers. The articles ranged from small, intricately made buttons and brooches to ashtrays, vases, powder bowls, clocks and candlesticks; but probably the most popular souvenir taken home to be displayed on the mantelpiece would be a cleverly turned and polished lighthouse. The making of these needed great skill, the details of which, handed down from father to son, were kept a great secret.

Over the past hundred years the majority of men who worked at 'turning' throughout the winter were village born and bred. The names Bosustow, Casley, Curnow, Hancock, Harris, Hendy, Hill, Johns, Jose, Leverton, Mitchell, Mundy, Olivey, Pascoe, Pitman, Richards, Roberts, Shipton and Williams immediately conjure up pictures of men long gone, and of their shops, many of which no longer exist.

The serpentine industry has unfortunately proved to be short lived as a family tradition, seldom extending to a third generation. This is due partly to an increased scarcity of stone, particularly the red, and partly to changing expectations in life-style. The lathes have been electrically driven since the 1960s, but the work is still hard and demanding, and the locating and quarrying of 'turnable' stone is becoming evermore difficult.

Today in the 1990s only six men are working full-time as 'turners' ~ Vivian Bosustow, Michael and Ian Casley, John Hendy, David Hill and Derek Pitman. Although small deposits of serpentine are found around the world and there is a sizeable one in New Zealand, it has only been worked commercially to any extent on this peninsula. The Lizard is famous for its serpentine. We hope that this will continue to be the case far into the future. *Compiled from information supplied by a number of serpentine workers.*

~ THE SOAPY ROCK MINE ~

'Soapy Rock' or Steatite, is a light coloured stone, soapy to the touch and soft enough to be crushed in the hand. It was probably discovered by the Cornish antiquarian, William Borlase, about 1740. He brought it to the attention of the potter, Josiah Wedgewood, who along with others such as William Cookworthy of Plymouth used it in the production of fine china until the development of more readily available china clay made the extraction of soapy rock uneconomic.

The soapy rock quarries at Gew Graze (Soapy Cove) lie just outside the parish and are all well documented. The work there, begun about 1750, is known to have been abandoned sometime before 1848, except for an occasional load needed for making Epsom Salts. What is much less well known is that there was at about the same time a Soapy Rock Mine within the parish of Landewednack on land belonging to Lord Falmouth. A lease granted by him to John Baddley and William Yates in January 1760 gave them 'free liberty license power and authority to dig and work a mine in and upon certain Veins and Loads of a Mineral Earth called Soapy Rock in the parish of Landewednack' within a 300 foot wide strip of land 'next to the Clift edge' and stretching from 'Gothillan (Caerthillian) Mill to Chynance in the north'. The rent was £12.12s a year plus a levy of £1.1s per ton of soapy rock above twelve tons raised. Exactly when the mine began we do not know, but by 1751 it was certainly in operation and doing quite well, for the financial statement sent to Lord Falmouth for that year shows that over 43 tons had been raised. This meant that Lord Falmouth and the three other shareholder-proprietors divided between them a levy of £32. 12s 5^1/$_2$d in proportion to their individual holdings in the 484 shares into which the mine capital was divided.

Sometime between 1760 and 1780 the right to mine soapy rock 'between a Cove and a Sandy beach by the name of Kinance and Cathillan Mill' was relet at £66 per year by its current owner Mr. Fonnereau. In 1781 its ownership became the subject of a legal dispute when the manor of Trethvas was bought by Christopher Hawkins. A letter from his Helston solicitor confirms Hawkins' claim to be the rightful owner of the 'Mine on Lizard Downs', it being within the lands he had purchased, and the dispute seems to have been settled in his favour.

We have no evidence though about what happened to the Soapy Rock Mine after that. Probably it shared the fate of the quarries at Gew Graze and was abandoned for lack of demand in the early part of the nineteenth century.   *Andrina Stiles*

~ ST WYNWALLOW AND LANDEWEDNACK ~

Not a great deal is known about St Wynwallow (or Wynwalloe), one of the most famous of the Breton saints. The earliest written evidence comes from a Latin 'life' written by Wrdisten, the Abbot of Landevennec in Brittany about 850, some 200 years after the death of St Wynwallow. It contains little in the way of hard facts and a great deal of pious imagining.

It seems, however, fairly certain that somewhere about the end of the fifth or beginning of the sixth century Wynwallow's parents (Fracan and Alba(?)) left their home somewhere in southwest England to escape a severe outbreak of plague. They sailed with their two sons, Weithnocus (Weithnoc or Wennoc) and Jacobus, across to Brittany where they settled on a large Romano-Gallic estate, deserted by its owners when Saxon pirates attacked the Breton peninsula. There a third son, Wingualeous (Wynwallow) was born.

By his own wish Wynwallow seems to have been early dedicated by his parents to the service of the church. So also probably had been his elder brother Wennoc. Wynwallow spent some years on the island of Laurea 'apprenticed' to a local holy man, St Budoc, during which time he gained a reputation as a miracle worker. Eventually he left St Budoc, and with some companions moved first to the island of Tibidy and then to Landevennec where he established an abbey noted for the severity of its ascetic life. (This was later moderated by the introduction of the Rule of St Benedict, which is still followed in the Abbey today).

According to an eleventh century copy of an early Abbey

Wooden statue of
St Wynwallow from the
Abbey at Landevennec ~

CHAPTER ONE ~ FOUNDATIONS

charter St Wynwallow died on 3 March, 'the Wednesday after Ash Wednesday'. Although the year is not known for certain it must have been around the middle of the sixth century. He was buried in the original abbey church at Landevennec, but when this was replaced by a bigger, better one sometime before 850 his 'body was translated (ceremonially moved) from the little church to the great church where we keep it today' as Wrdisten writes. He adds, 'We celebrate his translation on 28 April to avoid the inconvenience of his festival falling in Lent'. Sometime in the tenth century St Wynwallow was officially canonised. His feast day has recently been revived in Landewednack and is now kept on the Sunday nearest 28 April.

When the abbey of Landevennec was destroyed by a raiding band of Norsemen in 913, those monks who escaped went to the abbey at Montreuil, 'where they were received with great honour' and provided with permanent accommodation nearby. We know from a French royal charter that the monks managed to bring St Wynwallow's body with them to Montreuil, along with some of his relics. These included a bell, with which legend said he called the fish of the sea to him. Statues and paintings in the Montreuil area often showed him with a bell in his right hand and with three fish rising out of the sea at his command. When the monks were finally able to return to Landevennec and rebuild the abbey there they did not take St Wynwallow back with them. He remained at Montreuil until in 1793, at the time of the French Revolution, his shrine was destroyed, his bones scattered, and the buildings of Montreuil sold off at auction.

The parish church of Landewednack which is dedicated to St Wynwallow, is thought to have been founded as a daughter church of the abbey of Landevennec by one of its monks. Although there is a legend that St Wynwallow came to Cornwall, there is no evidence at all that he ever left Brittany. It is however possible that his brother St Wennoc did travel to Britain, and this could explain the name Landewednack, which means the 'Lan' (the Celtic word for 'sacred enclosure') of Wennoc. A 'Lan' was always roughly circular and St Wynwallow's churchyard still fits that description; and the earliest form of the name Landewednack was Landewennec. *Andrina Stiles*

The Stone Cross ~

~ THE STONE CROSS ~

Like other Celtic lands Cornwall possesses a large number of stone crosses. The round-headed one on Cross Common is now very worn and its carvings are not as easily deciphered as they were when Langdon made his survey of 'Cornish Crosses' some 100 years ago. He shows the head as having on it a plain straight-armed carved cross, the bottom of which continues right down the shaft as two incised lines. On the back of the head is a plain incised cross.

How old this Celtic cross is and what its original purpose was can only be guessed at, for no one knows for certain. All sort of theories have been

16 THE LIZARD IN LANDEWEDNACK ~

put forward. Cornish crosses have been said at different times to have been way-side 'prayer stations', signposts showing the way across a moor or to church, or place where a coffin could be put down for the bearers to take a rest for a while. More recently they have been interpreted as memorial stones, marking places where a Celtic 'saint' or missionary from Ireland, Wales or Brittany lived and worked to convert the Cornish people to Christianity.

Landewednack's ancient cross used to stand, or rather lean, against the hedge bounding the field called Parc Growse at the top of the road leading down to Church Cove. After the Second World War it was moved to its present upright position on the opposite side of the road where its height of four feet eleven inches has been a little reduced by sinking the shaft into the ground.

Using the evidence of other field names found in the Tithe Apportionment Roll of 1841 ~ Parken Grouse (Field no. 231 in South Trethvas), Park Grouse (no. 404 in Tregominion Wollas) and Cross Widden (no. 696 in Trenoweth) ~ one investigator believes that there may have been three more crosses in the parish. Nothing is known about these crosses or what happened to them, supposing they in fact existed. Langdon does not mention them. One other ancient cross does exist in the parish. It is, however, not native to Landewednack, but was brought here early this century from Merther in the parish of Constantine. It stands today over a grave in the churchyard. *Andrina Stiles.*

~ THE CHURCH ~

The parish church of St Wynwallow in Church Cove was founded some time in the sixth century, but nothing now remains of the earliest building. The oldest existing part of the church is the Norman doorway. Most of the rest of the church is fifteenth century with some Victorian 'improvements' and a few modern additions, such as the electronic organ. The local serpentine is well represented both as building material, used externally for the tower and, as ornament, used internally for the pulpit and lectern.

An estimated 4,000 visitors a year, a number of them from abroad, come and see and, it is hoped, to find spiritual refreshment in this the most southerly church in mainland Britain. Many of the visitors sign the book in the church and their comments make interesting reading. A selection of recent comments can be found in *If Only Walls Could Talk* on page 102.

In its life St Wynwallow's must have experienced much, but unfortunately we know very little about its early history. One of the earliest surviving records is 'A True Inventory of the Goodes of the Church of Wyvalal' made in 1549. The government of Edward VI was chronically short of ready money and ordered the seizure of all ecclesiastical vestments and the melting down of most church plate on the grounds that such things would no longer be needed for the new Protestant services. Despite being defeated by the name Wynwallow, the clerk went on to list the church's belongings. St Wynwallow's seems to have been quite well off at this time, for the list includes a number of vestments of black damask and blue velvet, along with a cope, a surplice and 'four towels for altars'. There was also a cross, a censer and two pricket candlesticks, all made of latten (brass). In addition three bells were listed. These, unlike the other goods, escaped seizure, and although not named can be fairly certainly identified. One of them seems to have been the tenor bell, 'Magdalen', known to have been cast about 1540. Now damaged, it is still in the church. The others were almost certainly the fifteenth and sixteenth century bells, 'Saint

CHAPTER ONE ~ FOUNDATIONS

Nicholas' and 'Saint Anna' which form part of the present ring of six. Included in the clerk's list of valuables was also a silver chalice, but as every church was required by law to have one such chalice, St Wynwallow's was probably allowed to keep it. A few years after this inventory was made the church is known to have acquired a silver cup and cover. This survived until the 1980s when sadly it was stolen from the church safe. In 1645 there was a visitation of the plague and the bodies of those who died, including the Rector, Robert Sampson, were buried in the churchyard and the area railed-off to prevent possible spread of infection. About a hundred years later, so the story goes, the railed off part of the churchyard was opened up to bury a number of shipwrecked sailors, and the plague reappeared, although in a milder form; but this is probably not true, for until 1808 shipwreck victims were not allowed to be buried in consecrated ground. They were instead interred as near as possible to the scene of the disaster, as happened in 1721 to the 200 or so people whose bodies were washed ashore from the wreck of the *Royal Anne* and who were buried in mass graves in Pystyll Meadow.

In more recent times another plague beset the churchyard, this time Dutch Elm Disease. It struck the fine trees around the church, and they had to be felled.

So much for the building and the churchyard. What about the people of St Wynwallow's? A list of past incumbents since 1275 hangs in the church, but about most of the early ones we know almost nothing beyond their names. One who is less shadowy than most is Richard Bolham who became rector in 1404. He left his name on the font 'Dn. Rich Bolham me fecit' (Master Richard Bolham had me made) and it is thought that he was also responsible for ordering much of the other work carried out in the church at that time. In 1678 St Wynwallow's is said to have been the venue for the last sermon ever to be preached in Cornish. Some say it was given by the then rector, the Rev. F. Robinson himself, others that it was by the vicar of St Keverne. Did the rector of Landewednack hold St Keverne in plurality? It is quite possible.

As late as the early nineteenth century, many clergymen still found the income from just one parish was not enough to support a family, and often, therefore, held more than one living. They would pay curates (usually young and inexperienced priests) a small salary to look after the extra parishes. Like every parish church St Wynwallow's had a 'parish chest', probably the one which we know from the churchwarden's accounts was made for the church in 1683 at a cost of 15 shillings and six pence. In this chest important documents were carefully kept, including the licences issued by the Bishop to Landewednack curates. A typical licence dated

Interior of Landewednack Church in the 1920s before the plaster was removed ~

photo J. Hart

1822 agrees that the rector shall pay the curate, Edward Tippet, £80 a year and allow him to live in the Rectory (now Landewednack House) and make use of the garden, orchard and outbuildings. He was also to have 'the tithe of line fish', that is a tenth of the fish caught by lines and not by nets. By the time another curate, John Bagwell Creagh, was licensed in 1824 the salary had gone up to £90 per year, and he also had the 'surplice fees', that is the fees for marriage and burial services. Reforms in the church of England in 1838 prevented clergy from holding more than one benefice at a time, and curates licenced to Landewednack from this time onwards were appointed as permanent assistants to the rector not as temporary replacements.

Before their final abolition in the 1930s, tithes were an important part of clergy income. Until 1836 a tenth of the harvest of crops and animals had to be paid in kind to the incumbent each year by his parishioners. In that year the tithe was commuted into a money payment, and in 1841 the whole of England was surveyed by government valuers. Each parish received a map showing all the cultivated land liable to pay tithe, and a copy of the 'Apportment Roll' showing the amount of money due annually from each holding under the new system. The parish of Landewednack was assessed for a total payment to the rector of £260 a year, out of which, under an old agreement, he had to give nine shillings to the vicar of Ruan Minor.

Another part of the rector's income came from his glebe. This was land belonging to the parish church and set aside for the benefit of the current incumbent. In the early days he usually farmed it himself. Later he more often leased it out to one or more tenants. Landewednack glebe was quite extensive, stretching from the church right up to the centre of the village. Some glebe land had already been sold to existing tenants or for development before the 1980s when glebe land was finally taken out of the control of local churches and put into that of the diocese.

One of the duties of any incumbent or his curate is to see that the registers of baptisms, marriages and burials are properly kept. These parish registers were made compulsory in 1538 but Landewednack's do not begin until 1578 and until 1654 contain only baptisms. The marriage entries from 1754 to 1813 are missing. Some burial entries suggest great longevity among the Landewednack clergy and people. The rector, Thomas Cole, who died in 1683 is said to have been 120 years old and his sexton who died in the same year to have been about 100. In 1754 an old man said to have been 104 was buried. These figures may need to be taken with a pinch of salt for until 1836 when birth certificates were introduced most people had no idea exactly old they were and always spoke about themselves as 'aged about...'. As they got older the figure they supplied tended to become exaggerated.

The church was always important in village life, not only in spiritual matters but in secular ways too. It was for a long time the largest and most substantial building in the area and had by law to be kept in repair. The money to do this was raised through a local tax, the church rate, which was also used for repairing the roads. The churchwarden received the church's share of the rate, kept detailed accounts of how it was spent and presented them annually to the rector and the people for approval. Usually, but not always, the accounts were accepted without question. In 1681 the Landewednack churchwarden found himself in trouble, for someone else has written at the bottom of that year's account, 'When this was read in church on 20th November the minister and parishioners would not allow it but protested against it and especially about the extravagant expense of the Bishop's annual visitation (18 shillings and six pence) and the cost of mending the church windows (five shillings)'. The churchwarden, who seems to have been suspected not just of overspending, but of fiddling the books, was forced to repay to the church

CHAPTER ONE ~ FOUNDATIONS

the substantial sum of 11 shillings. A year later there is another note in the account book. This one, elegantly written, strikes a sad note for it reads, 'And since I have lost my own true love, How can I choose but mourn', and is signed John Moor, Rector.

Throughout the last three decades of the 17th century the accounts are concerned with substantial restoration work to the church, mostly it would seem concerned with re-roofing. In 1674 when the records begin and Richard Williams was churchwarden he detailed his negotiations with the hellier (roofer) and carpenter. The work required the purchase of 2,000 'helling stones', which along with the necessary lime, timber, sand and several thousand nails, were transported by water as far as Gweek and had to be fetched from there by horses especially hired for the purpose. The bells were also in need of oil, ropes, collars, and new timber frames. These two items, the roof and the bells, along with the windows (which let in the rain, lost their glass, needed new bars or required expensive repairs to the stone surrounds) continually troubled the churchwardens during the next 100 or more years. Then as now, Lizard storms caused havoc from time to time, necessitating emergency repairs and the hire of men who had to be provided with beer as well as high wages of 4d 'for mending of the church being broken'.

We also hear of less serious matters which give us some idea of church life two or three hundred years ago. A contribution of 12 shillings and seven pence towards the rebuilding of St Paul's Cathedral after the Great Fire of London is recorded as being raised by the taxable landowners in the parish. Bottles of brandy were bought for the ringers at two shillings a bottle in 1697 when the peace was proclaimed which ended the long war with France, and 10 shillings was spent in celebration when King George I was crowned in 1714. The ringers also rang and were entertained at the church's expense on 5th November each year. Money was paid out to men and boys for catching vermin ~ foxes, hedgehogs and squirrels ~ at so much a head or tail. Over the years there were purchases of a Bible and a Prayer Book, a carpet, a flagon, a neatly framed board with the Ten Commandments and another with prohibited degrees of marriage, two deal benches and a linen altar cloth. Holy Communion was only celebrated three times a year ~ at Christide (Christmas), Easter and White Sunday (Whitsun) ~ and on each occasion the churchwarden had to ride into Helston to fetch in person the bread and wine needed. We do not know how many people attended church on a regular basis. One of the few pieces of information we have is that in 1812 there were 14 communicants out of a population of 303. The Churchwarden also had to obtain the soap with which the 'church clothes' received their annual wash, and the brooms with which the church was swept out once a year and the internal walls afterwards limewashed. Occasionally the churchwardens gave out money to the poor ~ a penny to an old soldier, another to a poor man from 'Tanjear' ~ but poor relief was normally the responsibility of the Overseers of the Poor.

From the sixteenth century onwards, before the establishment of any national system of local government, suitable parishioners able to read and write, were chosen to act as government agents. Each parish had to find and appoint two men as Overseers of the Poor. Their job was to collect the local Poor Rate used to support with goods or money any paupers who had a legal right by birth or marriage to live in the parish. At the same time the Overseers were expected to get rid of any poor who properly belonged to some other parish.

In Landewednack as in most other parishes churchwardens were often also Overseers of the Poor and their records survive from the late seventeenth century when most poor relief was in the form of goods. The early records detail food ~ usually meat or bread; clothing ~ usually shoes, or

Landewednack Church with stile and gate ~

A. Ellis

canvas smocks and shifts, occasionally stockings or a hat; household goods, particularly canvas bed sheets, and most often of all, payment of house rents or repairs. By the nineteenth century the situation had changed very little although rather more cash grants were being made ~ £1.17s was paid out in the second half of 1815 to villagers in need. Not all accounts were kept up to date. A small slip of paper gives details of a leg of veal, a shoulder of mutton and some calves' offal (total cost 13s. 17d) provided for an invalid via the Rector in May 1815; but a receipt was not obtained from the man's wife until three years later in March 1818.

Much of the Overseers' work was concerned with arranging for paupers to be removed to other parishes. Paupers had first to make a sworn statement to two Justices of the Peace, (who might also be Churchwardens and Overseers of the Poor) giving information about their place of birth, work experience, family and financial status. Some of these depositions make sad reading. From them the JPs decided which parish a man or woman rightfully belonged to and if necessary ordered them 'to be conveyed there out of hand'. This could be quite an expensive business for it had to be arranged in due legal form. A solicitor's account of 1819 shows charges of half a guinea for writing out an order for removing a family from Landewednack and a whole guinea for arranging for them to be escorted to Penzance. The removal the same year from Landewednack to Mullion of the wife and children of a prisoner held at Bodmin turned out to be a particularly complicated case and ran up a legal bill for the Overseers of £2 ~ a very considerable sum at that time, but worth paying to avoid the greater expense of maintaining the wife and children for an indefinite time.

A unwelcome situation for the Overseers was having to receive paupers from other parishes for settlement here. One such case concerned a 68 year old widow who had been born in Helston but was now living in Falmouth, the parish of her late husband. He had been a sailor in a man-of-war for 40 years, and when he retired 'kept a boat' until he became ill and died. As he was the illegitimate child of a Landewednack man, the widow applied to the Overseers here for financial help. In 1837 Falmouth magistrates found out that she had been getting a shilling a week from Landewednack for some time and ordered her removal. An endorsement on the order, however, states that she is so ill that the removal to Landewednack must be temporarily suspended. The suspension was never countermanded so probably she did not recover, and the Landewednack Overseers were spared the expense of supporting her. We do not know.

The Churchwardens, Overseers and Justices of the Peace were kept busy in other ways too. They were responsible for dealing with illegitimate children born in the parish, tracking down the father, serving him with an affiliation order, and extracting money from him to support his child. In 1830 a payment of £2.15s was levied on a Helston shoemaker to defray the expenses of the birth of a female child to a Landewednack girl, and he was ordered to pay the churchwardens and Overseers a sum of one shilling and eight pence a week maintenance. If the mother decided not

CHAPTER ONE ~ FOUNDATIONS

to keep the child she was also to pay maintenance ~ in her case ten pence a week. Five years later another girl, who had abandoned her child and left the parish, had failed to pay the ten pence a week ordered for maintaining her male child. The local constables were ordered to bring her 'without fail' before the local JP, who happened at that time to be the Rector, where she would be 'dealt with according to the law'. Unfortunately we do not know what happened to her.

To reduce the charge on the parish, pauper children were found employment as soon as they were old enough. At about eight years of age, they were bound apprentice (indentured) to a local employer to 'serve him/her honestly, orderly and obediently'. Many Landewednack children, both boys and girls, were not put to a trade or craft, but indentured as 'covenant servants' to learn 'housewifery' or to work on the farm, in return simply for board and lodging and a new set of clothes once a year. An indenture of 1814 apprenticed a 'poor boy' to his father, a tailor. The Overseers of the Poor made a single payment of £6.15s in return for which the father agreed to maintain the child until he was 21 during which time no cost would fall on the parish. An apprentice could not legally leave until he or she came of age at 21, but where they were illtreated or overworked they often ran away before their time was up. With no work, no family and nowhere to live they usually became paupers, moved on from parish to parish.

There was also the need to collect various taxes ~ Land Tax, Income Tax, Game Tax, Assessed Tax and a number of other taxes. Parish collectors were appointed and given a schedule setting out the amount due from each landowner. The collectors were paid 'poundage', around one percent of the total amount collected, in return for which they were personally responsible for the credit worthiness of all cheques, and had to write their names on all banknotes as a guarantee that they were not forged. It seems a thankless job but there does not appear to have been any shortage of applicants for the post. The same names appear year after year on the long series of receipts still among the church papers ~ so there must have been some advantage to be had.

Since the introduction of the welfare state the church has ceased to be involved in all these interesting activities which brought it into such close contact with the people of the village. Life is much duller as the result. *Andrina Stiles*

~ EARLY HISTORY OF THE LIZARD ~

What do we know about the history of The Lizard? Quite a bit about the early days and about more recent times, but unfortunately not very much about what happened in between.

The earliest known reference to The Lizard is in 150 AD in a *'Geography of Britain'* by the Greek philosopher, Ptolemy. He gives two different names: Dumnonium Promontorium (the promontory or headland belonging to the Dunmonii, the local British tribe) and Ocrinum Promontorium, meaning a rugged point.

Not until nearly a thousand years later do we find the next mention, when in 1086 (twenty years after the battle of Hastings) William the Conqueror ordered a survey of England to be made for tax purposes. This survey, known as the Domesday Book, includes an entry for The Lizard which it calls Lusart, Lisart or Lusard. There one Richard was the tenant of one hide of land on which he kept four wild mares, three cattle, 20 pigs, 60 sheep and 20 oxen to pull the ploughs. He paid tax on half the land on which there were also six villagers, six smallholders and six slaves and all of their families. There was no woodland but there were about six square miles of pasture.

His land was worth 30 shillings, little more than half its value before the Norman Conquest.

Richard was the son of Thorold or Thorolf. These names suggest that Richard was of Saxon or Viking descent. His landlord in 1086 was the Norman, Count Robert of Mortain, who had been rewarded by William the Conqueror with estates all over Cornwall. Richard's father had been one of 17 'thanes', independent landowners, who before 1066 held between them 11 hides of land in The Lizard area. For some reason 'these thanes could not be separated from their land's and they and their heirs remained on it as tenants of Count Robert.

In the years which followed The Lizard appears in official documents and on maps as Lesard in 1302 and Lezard in 1451. Lizard Point is called le Forlond de Lysard in 1427, Lysart Point in 1540 and Lezarde Poynte in 1605. *Andrina Stiles*

~ THE OLD WINDMILL ~

From my window at Mile End, I had often noticed what I took to be a misplaced 'Martello Tower' near farm buildings on the edge of Predannack Downs. Although we have been coming to The Lizard for over ten years, we had only recently moved in to the area, and my local knowledge was a bit lacking in detail. The 'Martello Tower' is, in fact, the remains of an old windmill, one of only five still standing in Cornwall. To my up-country eye, the 30 foot tower, constructed of serpentine and elvan with walls four feet thick is unlike any windmill I ever saw; in my experience they have always been of brick or even of timber. The tower stands two miles north of Lizard village, just inside the boundary of Landewednack parish close to the south-east corner of Predannack Airfield. It is a quarter of a mile west of the main A3083 Helston/Lizard road and one mile from the sea at Kynance Cove.

On researching this oddity, I found that it is, in fact, over 300 years old and may well date back to mediaeval times, although the style of the building suggests that it was probably built about 1600. It is described as an 'old windmill' on the plan by Joel Gascoigne in the Lanhydrock Atlas of 1695. There appears to be no earlier record of it. Gascoigne's plan depicts the tower only, with no sails, so by 1695 it may already have been in disrepair. Thomas Martyn's great Map of Cornwall in 1748, however, shows a recognisable sketch of a windmill with sails, and a lease of May 31 1755, grants Richard Felly, yeoman of the parish of Grade, a 14 year tenancy of 'the windmill croft within the parish of Landewednack'. This lease can only have been for the use of the mill and its land, as there was at that time no dwelling-house on the site.

By the 1770s 'A Plan of Windmill Croft' produced for the new Lord of the Manor, Thomas Fonnereau, builder of The Lizard Lighthouses, shows that stonework was crumbling, and that although there were still sails, there was no

Old drawing of the Windmill

cap. A few years later in 1787 the mill was let to James and Phillip Charles and extensive restoration work was carried out in 1790. The date and the initials BH appear in two places on the masonry of the south doorway. Messrs Charles were succeeded by Samuel Polkinhorne who is mentioned in leases dated 1800 and 1803, the latter describing him as 'of Landewednack, miller'.

This period seems to have been the mill's best time and lasted for about 30 years, although there was strong competition from the water mills in nearby Mullion, Cadgwith and Ruan Minor. The last advertisement of its working life appeared in the Royal Cornwall Gazette on October 11 1828 as 'a capital stone tower mill, complete and now working on grist'. It was to be sold by private contract, but successive occupiers seem to have concentrated on agriculture and the mill was again neglected. In view of its exposed position it soon fell into disrepair, although the tower was from time to time re-roofed, as it was the most prominent sea-mark of The Lizard Peninsular. The Cornish scholar Charles Henderson found it in 1916 and again in 1930 with a wooden roof, although locals described it as having been roofless for many years.

In World War II the tower was used as a look-out for the Home Guard, but again deteriorated and by the 1960s its conical slate roof had collapsed. It was adopted by The Lizard Field Studies Club in the 1970s who capped the walls to protect them from the rain, but it is now again in disrepair.

Such is the history of this fascinating building about which there are many stories. It is easy to imagine how once it ceased its working life in the late 1820s it became very useful to the gangs of robbers who flourished in The Lizard district. There was at that time no magistrate nearer than Trelowarren and the benefits of the new police system took time to spread to outlying country districts. There was no proper road from The Lizard to Helston and farmers on their way to and from market had to run the gauntlet of robbers lurking among the bushes. The old tower served as an undisturbed storehouse for the villains, and stolen sheep and cattle were said to have been stored and even slaughtered there on their way to the coast and a boat to Falmouth. There is a cave near Gue Graze still known as Sheep Stealer's Cave. A sheepstealer is said to have been hanged and afterwards buried in the walls of the windmill, and another story tells of a man murdered there. Inevitably the mill is said to be haunted.

Run-down and lichen-covered, constantly buzzed by helicopters, today it looks out on to the small 'copse' of its sleek modern brothers at Bonython, who albeit for a different purpose, are still harnessing The Lizard winds. I doubt, though, whether they will still be there after 300 years!

My thanks go to Mr Bishop who has worked Windmill Farm for almost 40 years.

John Lancaster

~ THE ARMADA AND THE LIZARD ~

The Spanish Armada set sail from Lisbon on 30 May 1588, but strong winds scattered some of the ships and forced the remainder to seek shelter in the port of Corunna on 19 June. There the fleet revictualled and carried out repairs while waiting for the missing ships to return. The news that the Armada was in difficulties reached the English Admirals who sailed out of Plymouth on 18 July to attack the Spanish fleet while it was still in port. The wind was against the English fleet and, apart from a number of small ships left as scouts in the Channel, the English ships returned home, arriving in Plymouth on 22 July, the very day on which the Spanish Armada set off at last for England, with favourable winds to help them.

A fresh gale on the 27 July scattered some of the Spanish ships, but these rejoined the Armada off The Lizard which was sighted at 4pm on 29 July. Meanwhile the Spanish had been sighted by one of the English scout ships. It speedily returned with the news to Plymouth, where skillful seamanship enabled the English ships to leave harbour and be within sight of the Spanish fleet by the afternoon of 30 July. All that day the Armada was preparing for battle, and all that day the Spanish sailors could see through the mist and drizzle the beacons flaring along the Cornish coast as the Armada began to move slowly up the Channel.

There is some doubt among historians as to exactly where the first sighting of the Armada was made but most would now say that it was from the Rill at Kynance. There is some uncertainty too about whether the news was passed by beacons at all. More prosaically, it may have been carried by messengers on fast horses. No such historical quibbles were, however, allowed to interfere with The Lizard's great day in July 1988 and the 400th anniversary Armada celebrations.

These celebrations included the employment of a spectacular pageant of floats organised by a large group of enthusiastic and hard-working people in the village, depicting various scenes from the First Elizabethan England. Not least was a wooden replica of Francis Drake's 'Golden Hinde' skillfully built over many weeks by a willing team of men.

Throughout the day thousands of people poured into the village, many hundreds having travelled from beyond the County. The entire square and Village Green were taken over by numerous stalls and entertainments ~ these to suit all ages and tastes ~ the actual number and variety defying description.

People picnicked or queued for food, as the case might be ~ by the end of the day the local shops were empty. The Smuggler's Fish and Chip Shop even had an extra delivery of fish from Newlyn, so great was the demand!

Many people came especially to buy the First Day Covers ~ The Lizard Village then having its own post mark, an unusual feature in itself for so small a village. Over 2,000 stamps were sold on the actual day and a further 1,000 went to dealers around the country.

Above all there was a general atmosphere of joyful celebration which did not decline with the weather ~ many people even resorting to 'wearing' dust-bin liners, thus offsetting increasing dampness as time progressed.

Towards the late afternoon a procession formed and led by a Brass Band, the majority of floats, followed by hundreds of cars and people slowly made its way along the toll road to Kynance Cove. It goes without saying that all payments were waived on that special day.

It had been decided by the National Trust that the first Beacon should be lit above Kynance Cove on the cliffs close to the car-park for convenience. A frigate from Plymouth would anchor close in, replying to the flare of the Beacon with a salvo from its guns.

During the evening the crush of the cars was so great along the narrow toll road that a 'tail-back' of traffic blocked the main road to Helston for many miles. The Spanish Ambassador who had been invited to light this symbolic beacon, was himself temporarily held up by this same traffic jam!

It has been suggested that above five to six thousand people reached the cliffs above Kynance by 11o'clock on that memorable evening. (Many hundreds however, did not arrive in time, being stranded on the approach roads.) But the Beacon was ceremoniously lit; the ship's salvo was heard in reply and a fabulous Firework display was then seen and enjoyed by all. Even the unfortunate presence of a thick, wet sea mist obscuring any possible view of the frigate, failed to dampen anyone's enthusiasm.

Over the next ten days history was further re-enacted by the lighting of a series of beacons stretching from the southern-most village in England and culminating with Queen Elizabeth II lighting a beacon at Windsor ~ this all being watched by many millions of people on television throughout Europe.

The united efforts of the entire community made that day a truly successful occasion for everyone, whilst left many happy memories, it was a day to look back on with justifiable pride by all those involved. The commemorative 'Armada Day' mug was just one of the mementos which many local people now value.

:Later that same year British Telecom erected a beacon strategically close to one of their 'dishes' at the Earth Station on Goonhilly Downs, to symbolise the 'first and last' in technological communication!

Our 1988 Beacon is to be permanently sited in a corner of the Village Recreation Field, marking the traditional place of the original 1588 beacon which is said to have been lit over 400 years ago to signal the arrival of the Spanish Armada. *Andrina Stiles and Derry Dobson*

~ POPULATION FACTS ~

1086 ~ Population of Lusart ~ Domesday Book
6 Villagers, 6 Small Holders, 6 Slaves, allowing for approximately 4 persons per household = 72

1522 ~ *19 Landowners, 12 persons owning goods worth £2 or more at approximately 4 persons per household = 124 (plus unknown numbers without goods or land)*

1812 ~ Population of Landewednack = 303

1821 ~ Population of Landewednack = 387

1831 ~ Population of Lizard Town and Church Town
194 Males and 212 Females. 78 houses ~ 8 unoccupied ~ 2 being built. approximately 4 persons per household = 406

1851 ~ *212 Males and 218 Females. 90 houses ~ 6 unoccupied. approximately 5 persons per household = 430*

1881 ~ *277 Males and 308 Females = 585*

1992 ~ *390 houses ~ 52 unoccupied Average of 2 persons per household = 803*

1995 ~ *403 houses ~ 57 unoccupied Average of 2 persons per household = 780*

The Lizard Village is quite unique ~ bounded as it is on three sides by the sea, the population has not increased as much as in other villages. Apart from seasonal tourism, second homes, transport problems and lack of work opportunities tended to check the natural growth of its resident population.

Despite the 'above average yearly temperature' ~ the village lying in the same latitude as the Isles of Scilly ~ the exposed situation and frequent high winds have been said to be a deterrent for many people in taking up permanent residence. Nevertheless, the 'locals' consider it the best and only village in which to live. *Edwin Carter.*

CHAPTER 2

The Land

~ CHURCH COVE ~ LANDEWEDNACK'S ANCIENT CENTRE ~

With true Lizard eccentricity, the village has not one but two hearts. The better known to holiday-makers and day-trippers is the area around the Green, with its pub, shops and parking. But, more discreet, more secluded and more venerable is the village's other core, half-a-mile to the East beyond The Beacon and Beacon Terrace.

At the end of the road lies Church Cove, the ancient centre of Landewednack parish and the original bearer of the name 'Lizard Cove'.

But before going down into the Cove and delving into its history, two 'disclaimers' : the ancient church itself is the subject of another chapter in this book, so will be mentioned only in passing here; and, although the name 'Church Cove' has come to be used for the whole area east of Cross Common, this chapter concentrates on the old, 'true' cove from the cluster of cottages around the church down to the sea.

First-time visitors rounding the sharp bend in the lane between Churchtown Farm and the church are inevitably struck by the unlikeliness of it all. Behind them lies the bleak wind-swept ruggedness of The Lizard plateau and the cluster of buildings known as Lizard Town. But suddenly, here are thatched cottages, fuchsia laden gardens, the warm hum (for most of the year) of bees, and a gently winding lane down to a tiny natural harbour. Tranquillity, not awe-inspiring grandeur, is the main impression here.

Church Cove IS different and separate, and always has been. Edwin Carter, who has known the Cove all his life, remembers when Churchtown people called their neighbours Lizard Onions!

Less than 200 years ago, there was not even a cart track between the cove and Lizard Town. Early 19th century commuters between the two communities had to trudge all the way up to the point where the modern A3083 forks near the Kynance Road, and from there back down to their homes or work. The linking road ~ Beacon Terrace ~ was not cut through until the 1800s.

But even Church Cove has seen changes, the most dramatic brought not by tourists or traffic, but a tiny insect. Until the 1970s, the head of the valley was an enclosed, heavily treed place with a cathedral archway of elms from Morwenna (now a nursing home) to the church. The church itself was virtually invisible behind its own cloak of elms, with only the four topmost turrets of the tower showing above the green canopy.

According to Edwin Carter, 400 elms were killed by Dutch Elm disease. Since then, hundreds more trees of various species have been replanted in blocks around the top of the valley ~ most of them by Edwin himself ~ but the landscape and its wildlife have been permanently altered. Not totally for the worst, perhaps: many people prefer the light and openness of the 'new' Church Cove, even if the winter storms do strike harder now, without that shield of trees!

Even so, the houses of the cove are still among the most sheltered in the village; the very age of some of them bears witness to the canniness of their original builders. The hamlet really starts at the farm, which dates back to the 12th century. In the last century, the Jose family ~ 22 strong ~ lived here. Lighting was by tallow candles; work, whether on the farm or cooking, mending or making clothes, filled the hours; the nearest doctor was in Helston, so homegrown herbs were kept as every-day medicines.

And, early in the 1800s, there was the added excitement of threatened Napoleonic invasions. A stock of pikes was kept at the church to fend off any foreign enemies attempting to land in the cove.

In more modern times, war did come in a semi-detached way to the cove: a German parachute was found hidden in the gorse on one of the fields belonging to Churchtown farm, near the main road at Cross Common. By then the farm had been taken over by the Stevens family, who are still working the farm on traditional lines in the 1990s.

The farm may once have been two separate enterprises; it is unusual in having two 'mowhays' (farmyards) either side of the current farmhouse. Such is the clutter of buildings on the site, with attendant cottages set at different distances and angles from the main house, that a two-farm set-up seems the most likely explanation.

Today, two thatched cottages join the farmhouse. They date back to the 16th century ~ the date 1569 has been found carved on one of them ~ and are now known as Wynwallow Cottage and Church Cottage. But according to Edwin, who lives in Wynwallow, they were once whimsically called What O and Who Cares ~ while the cottage opposite, now Trewidden, was known as Wy-Worry...

Two more thatched homes used to stand behind them, by the now leafy lane which runs alongside Church Cottage. They burned down, a common fate for old thatched homes in the 1940s. Two other thatched cottages have also gone. One stood between Parnvoose and Elm (now Grandad's) Cottage. It became uninhabitable during the Second World War, and was pulled down. The space where it stood is now parking for Parnvoose. The other, further down the lane, fell victim to fire in the early years of the 20th century. In its place now stands Solheim.

Dutch Elm disease apart, the years between 1920 and 1940 saw perhaps the greatest visible changes to Churchtown in its long history, with a small building boom which left the cove looking, architecturally, much as it does today.

Thatched Cottages in Church Cove ~

photo J. Hart

The big house next to the car-park below the church, Trevenwith, was built by an academic named Griffiths in this period; the now pink-washed Gue Gassel, below Parnvoose, appeared in the late 1920s; Solheim, too, dates back to the 1920s.

The gentle beauty of Church Cove has attracted visitors for generations, well before car-borne

CHAPTER TWO ~ THE LAND

traffic brought today's familiar influx. Until the Second World War, two pleasure steamers, the Queen of the Fal and the St Mawes, would bring mainly well-heeled visitors from Falmouth. They would transfer into rowing boats, step onto the beach ~ or clamber over Voose rock in the middle of the cove ~ then walk up the lane and on to Kynance.

With the hindsight of another half-century's knowledge, we will join them on their walk as far as the top of the hill, fill in some of the detail of what they must have seen, and highlight some of the changes between then and now...

Those changes begin even at the water's edge, and not just because of the disfiguring presence of the sewer-pipe, built in the 1960s. The cove was for centuries a sheltered natural haven for small fishing boats and for bathers. But during the Second World War, it was barred and fortified against invasion. With no maintenance on the slipway, the sea and storms did their worst. Then came the obtrusive concrete ugliness of the pipeworks and, however attractive the cove seems today, to local eyes it has never been the same again.

A cluster of buildings guards the cove. First, coming from the sea, is the old lifeboat house. It was an ill-chosen place with a difficult sea access and awkwardly sited, and soon became a store for boats and their equipment.

At the top of the slipway stand The Cellars, once a hive of local industry. A small pilchard fleet of seine boats was based in the cove, each carrying 16 men. A watcher on the cliffs, known as the 'huer', scanned the sea for pilchard shoals, and would alert the waiting crews. The boats surrounded the shoal and scooped up the fish in a huge net, or 'seine' before returning to the cove.

There the fish were salted and left in bulk. Later they were barrelled. The wooden beams which gave leverage to squeeze out the oil can still be seen set as a waist-high inverted shelf in the walls of the main building of The Cellars.

The pilchards are now long gone, and the various buildings of The Cellars ~ fish store, winch house and the rest ~ are today private dwellings or second homes.

Overlooking the Cellars is The Mariners, a thatched house with more stories ~ and storeys ~ than most. It has its own architectural interest as a comparatively rare old three-storeyed thatched dwelling. But The Mariners has also seen many changes. In its time it has been village pub ~ Mrs Irene Jane, now in her 80s, remembers her grandmother talking about the old inn sign ~ and one, two and even three separate homes, with the section nearest the sea known as The Swallow's Nest.

The building originally stood on a sort of early traffic

Trippers waiting on Battleship Rock in Church Cove to board the Queen of the Fal' returning to Falmouth c 1905 ~

photo J. Hart

30 THE LIZARD IN LANDEWEDNACK ~

island, with lanes front and back. In its inn days, drinks would be served through a hatch and placed on a counter outside so that horse-riders could take their pints without even having to dismount ~ a sort of early drive-in take-away! Even in the late 1990s, hops could still be seen growing above the path.

Mrs Jane's cousin Vivian Bosustow, whose family's serpentine stone workshop has been a feature of the cove for generations, tells how their grandfather was one of the serpentine turners who worked at the famous ~ but now vanished ~ Poltesco factory at Carleon Cove between Cadgwith and Kennack. He would walk from Church Cove to Poltesco and back for a day's work...

When Poltesco closed, Vivian's grandfather set up his own serpentine workshop in what is now the small holiday bungalow opposite The Mariners.

Like so many beautiful big old houses, The Mariners has had its share of notables. Noel Coward stayed there in his youth ~ and worried, it is said, about being teased with live crayfish by Granny Bosustow! After the Second World War, the popular radio comedian Jack Train bought the property as a holiday home.

Moving up the lane, those steamer voyagers would have seen village pumps and even a thatched pigsty near the thatched Cove Cottage. And then as now ~ from around 1919 onwards, anyway ~ they would have looked in at what is now Vivian Bosustow's tiny serpentine stone shop, which has a story of its own.

The impeccably-kept little stone specimen shop is actually older than Solheim or Gue Gassel, its stone-built neighbours. It began life as a meat-store at Bonython Air Station, known as R.N.A.S. Mullion, provisioning Royal Navy personnel during the 1914-18 war. When the war ended, Vivian's father had it delivered to the site on which it has stood ever since. A local haulier, whose daughter Ruth Barratt, granddaughter of a previous Rector of the Parish, still lives near the cove, did the honours.

Solheim, the distinctly Nordic name of Vivian and Freda Bosustow's house, commemorates an old act of kindness. Vivian's other grandmother, Mrs Champion, and her children were ordered to quit their tied farm cottage when Mr Champion was sent off to fight in the First World War. A Norwegian woman gave them shelter until he returned. Her home town was ~ Solheim.

The pink-washed Gue Gassel, built in the 1920s, was named after a coastal feature favoured by fishermen between Kilcobben ~ site of the modern lifeboat house ~ and Hot Point. Its first tenant paid £5 to live there...

Earlier steamer-borne visitors would have seen only open land here until they reached the thatched Parnvoose, where often a welcome cup of tea awaited on trestle tables in the lane. Rivalry in the cream teas trade is nothing new ~ Mrs Edwin Mitchell at Hansy Cottage, further up the lane, also catered to that early tourist trade with her jam and cream splits, saffron cake, heavy cake and even husband Edwin's homemade ginger beer... But on a hot summer's day, the long walk to Kynance and back in heavy dresses and suits must have meant plenty of trade for both Churchtown entrepreneurs!

Hansy Cottage, incidentally, was named after a ship of that name wrecked at Housel Bay in 1911. It had been carrying a cargo of timber and steel and for weeks afterwards, huge quantities of timber were washed ashore to find their way into local cottages ~ including the one now bearing its name.

At Churchtown proper, we have now come full circle and leave the steamer trippers to walk on, under the magnificent archway of elms, towards Lizard Town. Those trees, beyond doubt, mark the biggest visible changes between then and now. For with the death of the elms ~ and others including a magnificent Monterey cypress in the churchyard, uprooted during an easterly gale ~ much of the cove's wildlife changed, too. Barn Owls and Little Owls and many other species lived here. No more. But there have been compensations, like the thriving setts of badgers which have become a feature of the area.

Nothing is forever; everything changes in time. But at Landewednack Church Cove, to use its full mellifluous name, those changes have generally been slow and gentle enough to preserve the beauty of this, the most favoured corner of The Lizard. *Michael Lord*

~ KANGAROO IN THE COVE ~

Among The Lizard's wonderful wildlife, perhaps the weirdest appeared between the wars ~ a kangaroo. Owned by an ocean liner captain whose home was Morwenna, Church Cove, Joey lived in a special kangaroo house in the grounds. He was not an easy guest to handle. On one famous occasion Joey got loose during a rather fine tea party, leapt on to the dining table and wrecked all the fine china... while pocketing (or pouching) some of the silverware. *Michael Lord*

~ KYNANCE COVE ~

I suppose my earliest memories of Kynance would have been gazing up at a clear blue sky whilst being trundled along in a seventh-hand, hand-me-down Silver Cross pram, being jostled vigorously by my Mother from our home at Mile End, across the Downs. Having seven children, five of school age, the daily trip to the beach in good summer weather no doubt provided a much needed respite for my Mother from bored children.

Later of course I would make my own way, following the well worn track left by the coal lorries carrying their much needed cargo to fuel the generator at the Cove, which in turn left rich pickings as lump after lump would topple from the flat-beds ~ providing us with warmth through the bleak winter months!

The track would head out across the desolate moor towards The Ministry of Defence Site connected with Predannack Airfield (or the '*bottle*' as we knew it), a wooden structure with 12" walls packed with gravel and laminated windows of 4" thickness (which came in most useful as a milk bottle stand at the end of our garden). The centre of this structure had a spotting scope and a small external platform at the top. Although there in the sixties, the concrete base is now the only evidence of its existence. From here the path swung right towards the 'Quarries' where serpentine stone was dug for 'turning' in the souvenir shops in Lizard Town.

From this vantage point one can feel the abandonment of civilisation. Although farming of the Downs had been tried, only partial success had been achieved at Grochall Farm ~ 'Grochall' probably coming from the Cornish 'grughall' meaning a heather moor ~ the rare Erica Vagans growing abundantly on Kynance Downs.

Away to the right on the horizon are the remains of a windmill, one of the oldest in Cornwall, and described fully on page 23 of this book. Although used as a productive windmill from time to time, it is probably most notorious for its use by a gang of sheep stealers who operated on the peninsula during the 1820's.

One particular incident ~ the theft of four fine rams from the farm of Mr. Silvester about half a mile from Helston ~ in February 1829 led to the arrest of Alexander Hocking from Grade Parish and James Jose from Landewednack. In Jose's house, 82 lbs. of mutton, cut up and salted, some being concealed within a bed, were found. At Hocking's house ~ a butcher ~ two legs of mutton and some sheep skins were also found.

Once apprehended Hocking gave hints which involved Stephen Jose, who was brother to James, and William Harris. A party of 40 persons were assembled and led by Mr. Andrews ~ an active constable of Helston ~ chase was given across the downs towards Kynance where, all retreat cut off, Jose and Harris plunged into the sea. Being expert swimmers it is supposed they expected to reach some of the caves, but despite a boat search they were never seen again. In one of the caves near that spot the skin of the largest of the stolen sheep was found.

It transpired that the gang had been using the mill to slaughter the stolen sheep. From there, the fleeces and meat were taken to Sheep Stealers Cave just this side of the Rill and from there shipped to Falmouth. In spite of the evidence, a jury acquitted James Jose and Alexander Hocking. Hocking, having turned King's Evidence, cannot have found his position too agreeable on returning to the Peninsula. A field near the Windmill called 'Oliver Tucker's Grave' (so called in 1840) is reputed to mark the place where the gang murdered and buried a man of that name who had previously given evidence against them.

Even today, despite the constant stream of motor cars along the Helston road, the windmill and the downs towards Kynance still have a sinister look, especially on a dull, grey windswept day in winter. It requires little stretch of imagination to picture the scenes of violence and lawlessness for which they had so unenviable a reputation a century and a half ago.

But on down the 'coal' track a path crosses to the left leading to The Lizard and to the right to Water Gate ~ sometimes known as Kynance Gate ~ and the 'British Village' inhabited during the Bronze Age ~ Circa 1200 BC, many artefacts from which can be seen at the Helston Folk Museum. This path was used by those living at Jollytown for supplies from The Lizard and also by the postman ~ a long walk solely to deliver the post ~ this being a postal round in its own right at one time.

Kynance Cove ~ the cottage on the right was once a watermill ~

photo E. Hart

Going on down from this high plateau one starts to see tantalising glimpses of the majestic rocks of Kynance. Over to the left across Goose Curtain Stream, once stood a prominent four-square house and a wooden serpentine shop. Here could be obtained much needed refreshment after the uphill trek from the

CHAPTER TWO ~ THE LAND

Cove. It was also a shipping landmark and despite the buildings now having been demolished, it is still marked as such on Admiralty Charts. In 1986 the National Trust acquired the carpark complex and the toll road which was built just before the Second World War. From the beginning, the toll road became the main route to Kynance Cove, the track across the downs being mainly the preserve of walkers and ramblers, although back in the early years of the century horse drawn vehicles and later, coaches and cars regularly used this track. The garage at Mile End was specifically sited near the entrance for the sole purpose of fuelling the traffic to and from the Cove.

The track is now joined by a path from the main toll road which meanders towards the valley bottom. Kynance derived from Kewnans, meaning enclosed valley, is a very accurate description of this valley. The track now follows the Dog Brook which fed the overshot watermill once sited at the end of the cottages, virtually on the beach. This worked until the mill pool burst its banks. The mill was possibly one of the 'three watermills of Mullyon' so described in the West Briton of 1824 although no sign of it appears on the tithe apportionment map of 1840. Later in 1848, an etching in the famous book, 'A Week at The Lizard' by Rev. C.A. Johns clearly shows the mill and the mill wheel, and the census of 1851 gives a John Chittock as then Miller. It should perhaps be explained that Kynance Valley marks the boundary line between Landewednack and Mullion Parishes but the right hand side, although strictly in Mullion Parish, is always regarded by local inhabitants as being part of The Lizard.

The miller's house later became a Boarding House known as Thomas's Hotel and the mill grinding wheels were used as door steps, one bearing a bench mark signifying 27' above sea level.

Slightly inland from the house can be seen the remains of the stable which once had a thatch roof much like the small souvenir shop at the base of the steps to the minor headland, or Bar Green, where it is said that Jenefer Jose, born 1810, was interred in what was probably the last unhallowed grave in 1830.

Past the house on the right with its bridge spanning the Dog Brook and the privately owned cafe on the Todden to the left, the full grandeur of Kynance begins to unfold with Lion Rock (Ennis Vean) guarding the left, and the 'Bishop' keeping things right!

Some may think that this is the back door to Kynance as most visitors arrive via the carpark, but spending every day of my holidays and weekends at the beach it seems to me that this is the only way to approach the cove. Although *'Lake's Parochial History'* states that 'Kynance is a place to be seen, to be painted, to be dreamed of, but not to be written about' ~ I shall try....

Straight ahead the view of the sea is blocked by Albert Rock, so named after the Prince Consort and the Royal children who landed there in 1846, one of the Roberts family swimming to the boat as it moored up.

Turning to the right you pass through corridors of serpentine rock to a 'second beach.' At one time you would have had to pass under arches to achieve this goal as C.A. Johns describes, but as reported in The Times of 31 October 1865, 'The famous arch of rock yielded to the fury of a storm early in the week'. To the left is the aptly named Toad rock, and further towards the sea the Pyramid or Goat rock, nestling in a recess there is a small pool, where my Mother spent much time and patience in teaching my brother and me to swim.

On arriving at the second beach you are met by the impressive Asparagus Island (so named because of the plant which grows there ~ asparagus officionalis). The island was at one time probably connected to the mainland as the fishing flints found there and dated by Ivor Thomas as to be around 7000 B.C. show.

Also to be seen are furrow lines said to have been made by a later attempt to cultivate the island. Half way up the south face of the island is a cave which opens the rock to the sea and in rough weather spews out water, hence its name of 'The Devil's Mouth'. To the south of the island and separated by a narrow channel is the afore mentioned Bishop Rock, and to the east standing four square to the wind and sea, is the Gull Rock. To the north of the Island are the famous Bellows and Letter-box ~ later named the Devil's Bellows and Letter-box. The former spouts out jets of water and the latter ~ if you dare get close enough ~ sucks a paper message from your hand; the ferocity of both is dependent on a 'good swell'.

Returning to the sands you are dwarfed by the Steeple Rock and in its shadow the smaller Sugar Loaf. Across the beach you can enter the Parlour Cave and exit through the Drawing Room. At the edge of the sands just beyond is the Lady's Bathing Pool, and as a reward for scrabbling another 100 yards over the rocks, the Mermaid Pool is reached, a favourite haunt for young people to dive or jump into from the surrounding rocks.

Back across both beaches and at the start of the steps leading to the car park, the massive cliff of the Tor Balk (or Tar Box, as it is so often corrupted to) oppresses you. The route now follows a new, somewhat precarious stone and gravel path to the lower car park. The once familiar granite step, which previously 'adorned' Helston's Meneage Street, has now sadly been removed.

In 1977 the Countryside Commission compiled a survey of visitors to Kynance Cove along with a sample questionnaire. Of the average 1,800 people visiting Kynance each day, about 81% actually visited the beach. Of these 22% used the beach for resting, 16% for sleep/sun bathing, 14% for swimming, 13% for photography, 10% for a picnic, 10% visiting shops/cafe, 7% for children's play, 5% to view plants and birds and 3% for other purposes. The main attractions were given as coastal scenery, sandy beach, cliff walks, plants and wild life. At the time of the survey, Kynance had an average winter temperature of 4.5C and one of the highest 'sunshine hours' in Britain with a mean daily maximum temperature in summer of 20C.

Kynance, considered by many as one of the seven wonders of the British Isles, with its glorious beach and scenery is, to me the most beautiful place in the world.   *Nick Pryor.*

~ LIZARD BIRDS ~

The fame of The Lizard goes far beyond its scenery, serpentine shops and maritime subjects. Every year, especially in spring and autumn, it becomes a haven for thousands of migrating birds, many of them among the rarest and most spectacular in Britain. And where the birds go, so do bird-watchers, adding a new breed of visitor to the usual crowds.

The Lizard tends to display its birdy attractions in the most unlikely places: Black Redstarts on the village green's litter-bins, a Serin in a garden ringed by houses, a housing estate Hoopoe, a Hen Harrier along the main road.

Richard's Pipits feeding with Black Redstarts on cliff-top set-aside, buntings and finches bouncing over the Cornish hedges, Wrynecks grubbing around in field corners ~ all are, if not every-day arrivals, usually annual regulars.

Because of its exposed position The Lizard is less well equipped to hold a wide range of breeding birds, but still has its quota of interesting all-year residents, from Buzzards to Wagtails.

CHAPTER TWO ~ THE LAND

Among the sea-birds that make their home here are Fulmars ~ small, stiff-winged, gull-like birds which are cousins to albatrosses. Blue-grey in colour, they can be seen in summer in neat little pairs around the cliffs.

And always, out to sea, Gannets can be seen streaming past or diving like arrows ~ their Cornish name 'sethor' means 'archer' ~ into the sea for their food. *Michael Lord*

~ LANDEWEDNACK FARMS AND FARMING ~

Landewednack is appreciably smaller than the average Cornish parish, measuring 2116 acres or 3.15 square miles. Its neighbours to the north are the parishes of Mullion and Grade-Ruan and to the east, south and west the sea. It is England's most southerly parish and is unique in that it lies entirely south of latitude fifty degrees north.

The landscape is one that, over hundreds of years, has been crafted by man but within the limits imposed by the wind, weather and, perhaps more than any other mainland parish, the sea. Ever since two thousand or more years ago when the Neolithic farmers first turned the turf on Asparagus Island, then joined to the mainland, farmers have developed this land, creating homesteads and fields, growing crops and grazing livestock. Even the 350 acres of un-enclosed Lizard Downs is managed by periodic burning allowing the ericas, for which the area is noted, to survive the encroachment of gorse and willow.

Open and common land was brought into cultivation in a very sporadic manner from the earliest times. Later, when the fast growing population was hungry for land, the poor serpentine soils edging Lizard Downs did nothing to change this pattern of scattered fields interwoven with those of neighbouring farms. Even Trethvas Farm, admired for its compactness and centrally placed homestead, was, until circa 1880, four separate tenements of dispersed fields.

In the mid-nineteenth century a total of 1557 acres was farmed, the remainder being Lizard Downs. There were thirty-five tenements, of which thirty-three had homesteads, averaging 42 acres and ranging in size from 3 to 128 acres. During the next hundred years opportunity was taken to unite smaller holdings to form larger compact units. However, even today consolidation is incomplete.

Until the end of the nineteenth century all land in the parish was owned by landlords, principally Viscount Falmouth of Tregothnan, Mr. Hawkins of Trewithen, Mr. Lyle of Bonython and Mrs. Agar of Lanhydrock. Some land adjacent to Lizard Downs and the main road, including Lizard Green, was held jointly. During this century some tenants have had the opportunity to buy their own land.

Hedges ~

Hedges, so much part of the English landscape, here in Cornwall are especially valued for their flora and wildlife. In Landewednack, apart from a short stretch of dry stone wall at Lizard Head and some turf on the Downs, they are the true Cornish type composed of a rab core with facings of stone, gleaned from the fields during their creation long ago, held together with earth 'mortar'. They are very much living hedges, home to grasses, flowers, hawthorn, blackthorn and, especially on the serpentine soils in the northern part of the parish, willow. On

'Double hedge' to Kynance ~

cliff-side hedges salt-tolerant tamarisk grow freely. The only trees of note were the elms which once surrounded the parish church.

A well built Cornish hedge is expected to be good for 150 years before repairs are necessary. Threat to the well-being of the hedge comes from cattle, rabbits and overzealous trimming. Cattle can cause severe damage when searching for juicy grasses or when driven mad by flies. Often a rubbing stone was maintained in the centre of a pasture for their convenience. These were removed this century to make way for modern machinery except for two highly polished stones still standing in fields beside Green Lane.

Rabbits not only eat valuable crops but, in large numbers, seriously weaken the fabric of the hedge by their burrowing. In times of poverty and food shortages, as in World War II, they were a source of cheap protein. However, they became such a serious pest that some tenants, encouraged by their landlords, engaged the Helston Rabbit Clearance Society to keep them under control. The Society employed three full-time trappers, one of whom was Mr. Charlie Bosustow from Mullion who came annually with his pony and trap. Even the outbreak of that dreadful disease myxomatosis in the 1950s failed to eradicate the problem. Organised trapping in the area ended on the cessation of government grants in 1971.

One type of hedge peculiar to Landewednack deserves special mention; the double hedge. It is approximately six feet tall, five feet at the base and no more than four wide at the top, along which runs a footpath. Four exist but only two are currently in use at Trethvas and Kynance. The Trethvas double hedge is on the path from Lizard Town to Grade-Ruan and, despite two acute double bends along its length, is very much a highway for pedestrians and careful cyclists. The Kynance path was, during the nineteenth century before Kynance Road was laid, the main route to that famous tourist attraction. At the far end of the hedge, where the land dips towards Caerthillian Cove, the Glen Cafe once offered refreshments to weary travellers.

The well-trodden steps to the double hedges, like the numerous stiles around the parish, have been brought to a fine polish over hundreds of years, but as most are serpentine, when wet are particularly slippery.

Hedges were not built for their aesthetic appeal. They had the three-fold function of acting as a receptacle for stone cleared from the field, for delineating the property and acting as folds and shelter for livestock and, conversely, for keeping animals out of cropped areas. In the earliest days the developer of the land had no wish to carry stone further than he had to. Consequently, the earliest fields, if we can call them that, were exceedingly small. In 1840

CHAPTER TWO ~ THE LAND

there were no less than 577 fields in the parish averaging 2.7 acres, probably few having changed since their creation.

Landlords, in their tenancy agreements, decreed that hedges should be kept 'in good repair, order, and condition'. A tenant had to make a strong case to remove hedges in the interests of better land management. Even so, losses occurred before such farms as Tregominion, Church Town and Trethvas were sold to owner-occupiers who were free to remove hedges as they wished. In the last one hundred and fifty years at least one quarter of the hedges existing in 1840 have been removed. There are now approximately 324 fields averaging 4.8 acres.

It is interesting to note that in 1840 there were no less than 75 miles of hedges representing an estimated 84 acres of useful wildlife habitat. Despite the loss of hedgerow and some conversion of croft land to pasture, Landewednack, with its Lizard Downs and cliffs, still boasts a varied and extensive habitat for wildlife.

Although it is not possible to date a field system with any degree of accuracy, it is possible, by map reading and studying field names, to get some understanding of the development of the landscape. The earliest fields were very small and irregular and there is evidence of this in the vicinity of Lizard Town and the church which has a Celtic foundation. The fields skirting Lizard Downs are squarer and the hedges run in straight lines. The Great Croft, to the west of Rose in the Valley, was, in the nineteenth century, the last common land to be enclosed, supporting the theory that the downsland tenements were the last to be created. It is noticeable that the field names are English whereas those around Lizard Town and the Church are exclusively Cornish. It is a remarkable fact that these Cornish names are still in use today. Park Bithian, Todden, Drea, Grouse, Brawse, Gollon, Carbis, Ventewidden, Caneer, Vortol ... Space forbids listing but a few. Their spellings may have been changed by scribes unaccustomed to the Cornish tongue but they all have their meaning and, importantly, they are alive today!

Farms and Farming ~

Farms started in a very small way and so it was with the farm buildings. Farmers in the eighteenth century had a few cattle, sheep, pigs and poultry and oxen or a horse as draught animals. This diversity limited losses in the event of poor market prices or disease. Also it suited trade which was conducted locally either for cash or barter. Accommodation for these animals and their feed ~ corn, hay and root crops ~ was modest. A good example is Gweal Crease which still retains its yard surrounded by a livestock house, barn with granary over and the dwelling house close at hand.

A typical dwell-ing house at Trethvas, now demolished, was built of lower stone courses surmounted with cob, a mixture of straw and clay, and thatch. Rooms, barely six feet high, were separated by lath and plaster walls. There was a kitchen, boasting a small Cornish range, a parlour and a scullery and three equally small bedrooms above. Outside in the garden the toilet was situated close to the pump. For all its modesty of size, it was a warm and cosy abode prettied in its time by rambling roses.

In the Victorian period there was a need for larger farms and dwellings to accommodate the larger families. Trethvas, once four separate homesteads, was rebuilt retaining few of the old buildings. It was designed around the central yard with the dwelling house now quite separate. It boasted an impressive range of accommodation for 7 horses, 15 cows, 10 feeding cattle, 8 bullocks, 8 yearlings and a piggery of 5 styes. A spacious barn of three rooms had steps rising from the large mowhay and there were spacious implement houses.

In addition to two cottages already in existence, a new much larger dwelling was built with no less than six bedrooms, two of which were served by a back staircase reserved for servants. A pump was conveniently placed in the back kitchen. Two toilets, one for the servants and the other, fitted with two seats to accommodate an adult and child, was discreetly placed at the back of the house.

Cutting corn with a binder and horses at Trethvas in 1930s ~

photo W. Hocking

Similar farms on the quadrangle principal were built at Tregullas and Hellarcher. Their function, good for ninety years, is now outdated by the need for greater specialisation. The agri-business of today requires accommodation for 70-plus herds of cows, integral covered sheds for fattening stock and for their feed. Vernacular architecture has given way to pre-fabricated wooden walled and metal-roofed structures with ample room inside to accommodate the tractors and machinery necessary for livestock management.

Life in the parish right up until World War II centred very much around agriculture. When Queen Victoria ascended to the throne there were 34 farmers, employing 22 boys or girls and 27 farm labourers. In total they had 176 dependants. Indirectly, the lives of a blacksmith, 2 butchers, a cordwinder and a wheelwright and their families depended upon the success of the industry.

Although Victorian farms were labour intensive it is not to say that they were without machines and labour saving devices. Most of the common implements, the harrow, sickle, scythe and spade, had been in use since before the Normans came to England. The all important plough, with coulter and mould-board, had changed little since William I's day although it had been improved to permit the turf to be turned in one direction, whether going up or down the furrow. Teams of six or eight oxen had given way to pairs of Shire horses as the motive power in this demanding work.

A man and his two-horse team would expect to plough approximately 2 acres and travel 20 miles in a day. Their progress would be marked by scores of seagulls vying with each other for the large juicy earthworms. Most of the ploughing was completed before Christmas giving the soil ample time to weather before the ground was worked to a fine tilth ready for drilling seeds in the Spring. In March, the soil was worked with a chissler or cultivator, harrowed and rolled.

CHAPTER TWO ~ THE LAND

Fertiliser was then applied from a seedlip, a kidney shaped wooden or tin box, suspended from the shoulder by a leather strap. It would hold three quarters of a hundredweight which was sown by hand in strips ten feet wide. The sower would mark his course by towing an old plough share behind him!

The ground was now ready to receive corn, turnip and mangold seeds, the staple crops (and hay) with which to feed the animals during the long winter months.

The corn seed was once sown in a similar fashion to fertilisers but the invention of the seed drill made a marked improvement in efficiency by evenly sowing the seed. Thistles were the chief threat to growing corn. Their deep tap-roots were laboriously removed using a paddle, a two inch blade at the end of a four foot hilt.

Spring was always a very busy time for the farmer. Cattle, which had been housed during the winter months, were turned out to pasture. Their houses were cleaned out and the resultant dung and straw carried by horse and cart to the grass fields where it was deposited in piles, eight or nine to the cartload, to be scudded or spread by a man using a four-pronged fork or heaval. Additional fertility was applied by the use of sand and seaweed drawn from local beaches and marl, a mixture of clay and lime, drawn from pits on the farm. Marl pit sites can still be seen at Hellarcher and Trethvas.

The hay harvest started in June. The horse-drawn hay machine was a major advance over the back-breaking work of cutting hay with a hook or scythe. Even so, the harvest still required the assistance of all the family, workers and seasonal workers. Once cut it was turned using the two-pronged fork or pike until dry when it was carried into the mowhay to be built into a rick. The hay was lifted to the appropriate place with the aid of a pole, grabs and horse. The pole was secured by four guy-ropes and canted towards the centre of the rick. The horse, guided by a senior or junior member of the family, hauled the load by means of a wire rope and series of pulleys to the required height. The load, suspended on a jib, was guided to the desired spot before the grabs were tripped by tugging a short rope.

Building a hay-rick required skill to avoid it settling with a lean, a situation likely to incur derision among the neighbours! Hay containing too much moisture could over-heat and even catch fire threatening the mowhay and homestead. Such a valuable crop might possibly be saved by cutting three shafts vertically into the centre of the rick to ventilate it.

The newly emergent turnips and mangolds had to be horse hoed but the intricate cutting out had to be done by hand hoe. It was boring relentless work.

The corn harvest, as with the hay harvest, required all hands, men, women and children, and good weather. Even in the twentieth century the scythe has been used. The sheaves were tied with a handful of reed and thumbknots. The binder, drawn by three heavy horses, bound its sheaves with twine and bevelled the butts to aid the building of shocks, mows and ricks. Six or eight sheaves were placed on end to form shocks where the corn would continue to ripen. The job of pulling in the sheaves was allocated to the boy whose bare legs by the end of the day were lacerated by the stubble, butt ends and thistles. In wet seasons the corn would be built into arrish or knee mows to finish ripening when it could be carried at a more convenient time.

By August the corn was ready to be carried into the mowhay. Usually two teams of horses and wagons were employed to fully engage the master builder. Care had to be taken in building the wagon as invariably its journey to the mowhay was a rough one. Although the wagon had riggers in front and behind, the load had to be secured with ropes tightened by capstans. Meanwhile the master builder took care and pride in building the rick. Once completed, it was thatched with wheaten straw and secured with twine weighted with stones. The ricks were built in pairs allowing sufficient room between for the threshing machine. In a fair season the harvest would be completed by mid-September.

Although the harvest meant hard work and long hours, the comradeship and sense of job satisfaction made for a happy period in the farming calendar. In rejoicing and thanksgiving, all would join in decorating the churches and chapels with all manner of fruits of the land for Harvest Festival and lustily sing *'We plough the fields, and scatter'*. Since the introduction of the combine harvester and baler in the 1950s, the romance and comradeship of harvesting has gone.

Although mechanisation might be considered to be a relatively modern phenomenon, it has been with us, albeit in a small way, for a very long time. The Domesday Book records water mills throughout the country and, although only two were recorded in Cornwall, they were certainly widespread later on. It seems likely that Landewednack had one or more.

A threshing and milling machine, installed in the barn at Gweal Crease, was driven by a horse walking around a capstan outside. A good example of a round house, possibly eighteenth century, constructed of stone and cob, which gave shelter to the horse and its handler, can be found at Church Town Farm. The nineteenth century saw considerable progress in mechanisation which, rather than saving labour, enabled farmers to increase productivity. The steam driven threshing machine was one such major innovation. The Erisey set, consisting of thresher and stationary engine, which Mr. Hendy of Tregominion engaged in 1890, was, at the end of a day, moved by two teams of horses supplied by the farmer whose work had just been completed. Luggs and The Meneage Threshing Machine Company invested in a traction engine relieving farmers of this onerous task. Nevertheless, the task of managing the machine meant long hours and dirty work during the short days of winter. The engine had to he fired up at 7 a.m. for a 9 o'clock start. Two ricks were threshed in a day finishing at approximately 5 p.m. when the set had to be moved on to the next site. Once the thresher and engine were aligned, the engine's fire had to be doused and water and coal made ready before retiring.

Threshing ~ pronounced locally 'thrashing' ~ days required a large labour force of nineteen men supplied by neighbouring farms in Grade and Ruan Minor as well as Landewednack. The men on the machine who cut the binds and fed

Hay harvest with a pole on a Landewednack farm ~

the drum had to be supplied with a steady stream of sheaves pitched by three men. The corn, in two hundredweight sacks, were carried by three men, giants of strength, up the steps into the barn. The bundling of the loose straw with thumb-bines required five men to keep up. Latterly a mechanical bundler made big savings . The straw rick had to be built and the chaff swept clear.

The hum of the machine ceased only for morning and afternoon crousts and midday dinner. These were times, as at harvest time, when the farmer's wife could excel herself with her cooking. She would bake white, saffron and heavy cake a day or two before but the splits had to be fresh with real butter. The slate farmhouse floors would ring to hob-nailed boots as the men went in to a dinner of meat, fresh vegetables, pies and fresh clotted cream.

Threshing days, despite the disruption to ordinary farming routines and the hard work involved, were savoured for the chance of swopping news from different farms and parishes worth a year's supply of 'West Britons'. It was a time to renew acquaintances, share jokes, boast a little of past achievements and relive old times.

The best of the corn was kept for seed but the bulk of it was milled for feeding the livestock. Wheat was grown for thatching and that used for buildings was hand threshed over a log of wood. Additionally, turnips were drawn direct from the field and chopped in the turnip house. Mangolds were clamped, usually against the side of a hedge, and covered in old straw and furze to keep out the frosts.

Cattle were reared for milking and beef, the produce being sold locally. The farmer's wife, who made a valued contribution to the agricultural enterprise, had the task of scalding or separating the milk for cream and butter. The waste, mixed with flour, was fed to pigs. Her other speciality was the poultry. She would rear and fatten chicken, ducks, geese and turkeys and prepare them for the house and local demand. Livestock, bullocks, sheep and pigs were fattened on the produce of the farm. In the nineteenth century they went to the local butcher who slaughtered them on the site near Trenoweth. When farmers produced more than was required locally, cattle were driven to market at Helston. The journey of eleven miles meant an early start and accepting the prices offered. One man is said to have withdrawn his cow due to low prices only to have her drop dead on their return to the farm!

Added to the hazards of disease and poor market prices was the possibility, albeit infrequently, of losing stock over the nearby cliffs. Uncontrolled dogs were the usual culprits although Mr. Hendy recorded in 1909 losing one of his best ewes as the result of the thoughtless action of a couple of boys. Cattle straying onto another man's land were impounded and only released on the payment of a fine. Field names suggest a pound sited at the head of Caerthillian Lane.

Sheep, by law, had to be dipped in a tarry solution to counter scab. This dirty, distasteful job was overseen by the village constable. The parish dip can still be seen at Gweal Crease.

Changes ~

Landewednack, geographically isolated from the rest of England, was transformed by the outbreak of World War II. Suddenly, the air buzzed with the strange accents of servicemen, land-girls and evacuees. The cultural differences of townspeople mingling with the rural community came as a shock to both sides but, in the face of the common enemy across the Channel, friendships were made some of which were to last a lifetime. The steady, measured tread of the gentle giants of the field, the Shire horses, was overshadowed by lorries carrying thousands of tons of aggregate, blasted, crushed and graded, from the quarry at Church Cove for the construction of Predannack airfield.

The pace of farm life quickened. Time-honoured crop rotations were abandoned in favour of increased cultivation of wheat, potatoes and sugar-beet to replace losses to the U-boat war. The United States of America early in the war provided agricultural equipment, principally tractors, to help Britain feed itself. It was the start of an accelerating trend leading to the highly mechanised, labour efficient, agri-business that we know today.

Among the first to benefit was The Meneage Threshing Co. which replaced its steam traction engine with a Case. The new machine speeded the movement of the set from farm to farm and dispensed with the need of firing up at the start of day. However, the threshing machine's days were numbered. The combined harvester, which cut and threshed at the same time making shocking, mowing, carrying and the building of ricks a thing of the past, replaced the set in the mid-1950s.

The hay harvest was transformed with the introduction of the stationary baler, the first of which was owned by Messrs. Wilfred and Harry Harris of The Lizard in 1948. The cost of the new machines and the need to fully employ them introduced a new concept in farming, that of contracting.

Also in the 1950s mains water, electricity and the telephone improved living standards for all. Outside toilets, less than convenient on wild winter nights, were replaced by indoor lavatories and bathrooms. Cows, once hand-milked by members of the family sitting on three-legged stools out in the yard, now enjoyed the comfort of customised milking parlours.

Countrywide markets made possible by the opening of Helston Railway Station in 1887 were further expanded in the post-war period by the building of better roads in the West Country. Farmers, taking advantage of the equitable climate to grow cauliflowers, broccoli and early potatoes, took advantage of the Hendys' haulage business to transport their produce door to door, bypassing the need of transhipment at the station.

The twentieth century has seen vast changes on the agricultural scene. Landowners, who had had land in the parish for hundreds of years, were forced to sell to pay death duties. Some sitting tenants were in an advantageous position to buy. The need to operate larger units in the face of increasing economic pressures, mainly from Europe, has seen the loss of farm names such as Harris's Tenement, Travellers' Rest and, recently Trenoweth. Many families like the Chittocks, Joses, Richards, Lynes and Hockings who had farmed in the area for two hundred years or more have left the industry.

The National Trust with their acquisition of Trenoweth, Tregullas and Tregominion, as well as considerable tracts of morrop or cliff land, are now a major land-owner in the parish. Their principles of conservation, and those of the Countryside Commission with interests in Church Town, will be the pattern for the future.

Older residents and visitors who came to experience life in a rural parish will remember the sunny days of old, the harvests, crousts, companionship and the dairy herd emerging from Chapel Lane making its unhurried way across The Green to be milked at the farm in the very heart of the village. Some will regret the passing of this way of life, its measured pace and its values. Farming, as any other industry, has undergone continuous change. It is not the change but the speed of change which is most alarming. *W.R. Hocking*

CHAPTER TWO ~ THE LAND

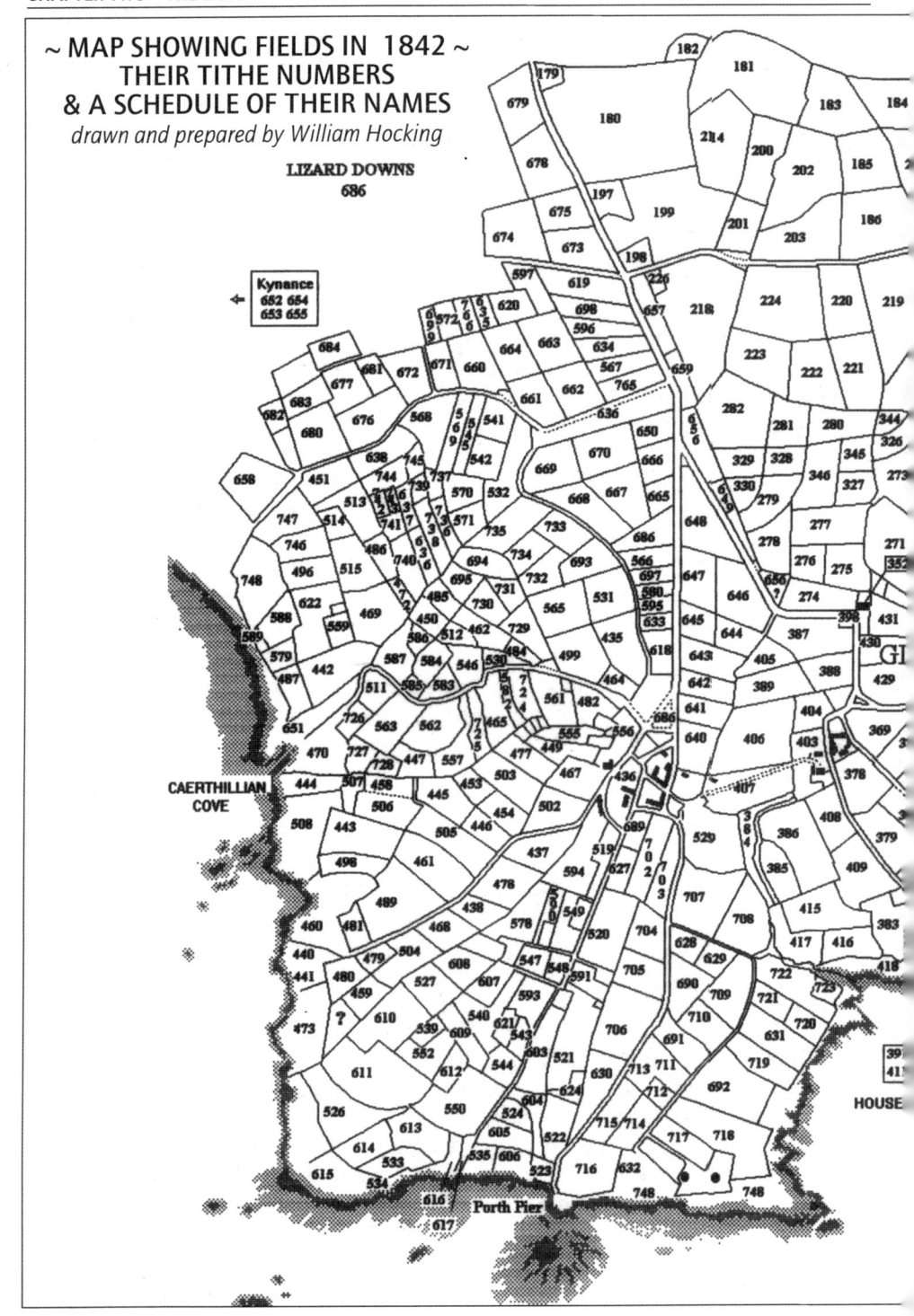

~ MAP SHOWING FIELDS IN 1842 ~
THEIR TITHE NUMBERS
& A SCHEDULE OF THEIR NAMES
drawn and prepared by William Hocking

CHAPTER TWO ~ THE LAND

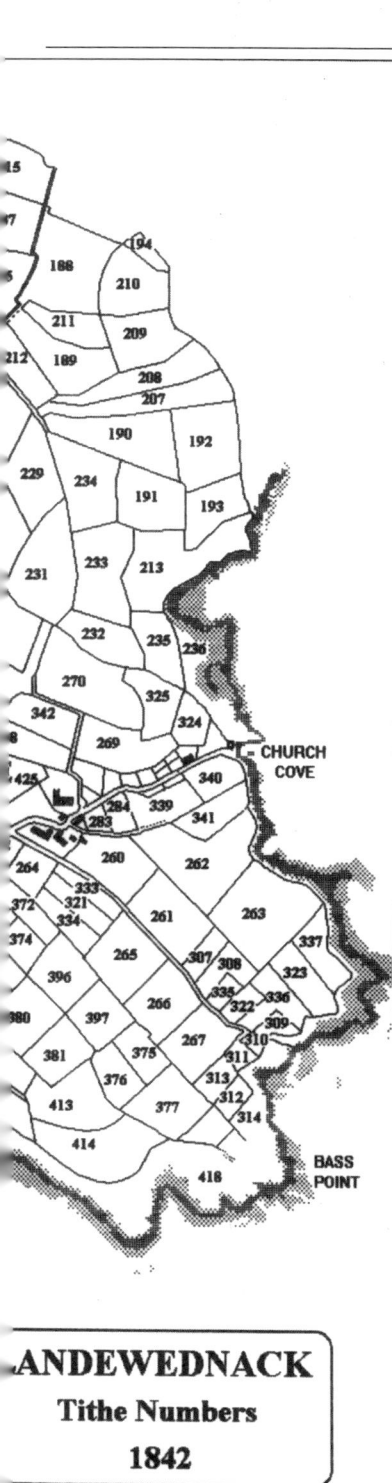

FIELD NAMES RECORDED IN THE TITHE SCHEDULE OF 1842

179 Croft Peggy
180 Downs Croft
181 Homer Croft
182 Middle Croft
183 Three Corner Croft
184 Hoverack
185 New Croft
186 Croft Margery
187 Park Todden
188 Park Bithen
189 Park Dray
190 Lelane Field
191 Higher Cliff
192 Lower Lelane
193 Lower Cliff
194 Moor
197 Downs Croft
198 Croft Jane
199 Great Down Croft
200 Little Park Broase
201 Way Croft
202 Park Broase
203 Por Bean
204 Cotton Peath
205 Cotton Mead
206 Garden
207 Long Lelane
208 Homer Lelane
209 Orchard Park Bithian
210 Kouneys Park Bithian
211 Little Park Dray
212 Great Park Dray
213 Cliff Field
214 Pool Croft
215 Hovenack
218 Gold Vians Croft
219 John Bougey
220 Higher Kilinmeer
221 Lower Kilinmeer
222 Park Dower
223 Park Caine
224 Park Yet

225 Lower Park Bithian
226 Park Betty
227 Poor Bean
228 Higher Park Bithian
229 Higher Polleno
230 Lower Polleno
231 Parken Grouse
232 Furse Hill
233 Great Cliff Field
234 Parken Bounder
235 Little Croft
236 Boa East
260 Laxon Dray
261 Outer Dray
262 Homer Goben
263 Outer Goben
264 Hale Wartha
265 Heskinninion
266 Higher Derese
267 Lower Derese
268 Gillear
269 Lower Park Gollon
270 Higher Park Gollon
271 Park Cairn
272 Park Ponds
273 Hallais
274 First Croft
275 Middle Croft
276 Lane field
277 Outor Croft
278 Digory Croft
279 Parsons Croft
280 Hale Mill Croft
281 Furrze Croft
282 Higher Croft
283 Well Meadow
284 Lean Meadow
302 Lodge Field
307 Higher Field
308 Middle Field
309 Water Field
310 Meadow

ANDEWEDNACK
Tithe Numbers
1842

~ THE LIZARD IN LANDEWEDNACK 45

CHAPTER TWO ~ THE LAND

311 Hill Field	383 Carbis	448 Meadow	510 Goss Garden
312 South Field	384 Daggs Moor	449 Nethenack Field	511 Toulson Hill
313 North Field	385 Lower Daggs	450 Cairn Mellin Croft	512 Cairn Mellin
314 Morrop	386 Higher Daggs	451 Cairn Goon	513 Carn Goon Croft
321 Cartheen Field	387 Outer Croft	453 Great County Hall	514 Little Carn Goon Croft
322 Ventewidden	388 Homer Croft	454 Little County Hall	
323 Hot	389 Park Todden	458 Anney Veryan	515 Lower Carn Goon Croft
324 Lower Park Bowls	390 Derene Moor	459 Cligger	
325 Higher Park Bowls	391 Willow Garden	460 Morrop	519 Park Praze
326 Hale Mill Field	392 Bongey	461 Creggo	520 Treglouse
327 Half Croft	394 Great Buck Field	462 Croft	521 Park Noweth
328 Lower Croft	395 Lower Buck Field	464 Park Pound	522 Water Field
329 Higher Croft	396 Homer Catheen	465 Vortol	523 Porth Pier cliff
330 Homer Croft	397 Higher Catheen	466 Meadow	524 Torhoddna
333 Homer Catheen	398 Barn Field	467 Park Dray	525 Park Bougey
334 Outer Catheen	399 Common	468 Cairn Braase	526 Lizard Head Cliff
335 Ventewidden	404 Park Grouse	469 Canalier	527 Darrow
336 Water Fields	405 Park Cathen	470 Copen Carna	528 Annadanner
337 Hot	406 Higher Caneer	472 Little Canalier	529 Meadow
338 Orchard	407 Lower Caneer	473 Morrop	530 Carn Mellin
339 Homer Lans	408 Higher Park Dray	476 Park Bean	531 Arraview
340 Lower Lans	409 Lower Park Dray	477 Coundy Hale	532 Trelvin
341 Higher Lans	410 Garden	478 Gaben	533 Pistole Cliff
342 Christevennas	411 Little Moor	479 Higher Rowles	534 Pistole Cliff
343 Park Pons	412 Lower Park Ebgar	480 Lower Rowles	535 Round Hill
344 Hale Mill	413 Higher Park Ebgar	481 Cregga	539 Park Mistress
345 Lower Croft	414 Carn Crobbin	482 Park Pounds	540 Carrick Widden
346 Higher Croft	415 Great Howzale	483 Park Todden	541 Telvin
349 Ventevorrian	416 Little Howzale	484 No Man's Land	542 Lower Telvin
350 Moor	417 Moor	485 Cairn Millin	543 Higher Park Bouggey
369 Park Dray	425 Lower Field	486 Lower Croft	
370 Long Field	435 Park Todden	487 Canalier	544 Lower Park Bouggey
371 Square Field	436 Park Bean	488 Rellenvillen Hill	
372 Guinea Field	437 Great Goben	497 Cliggar	545 West Telvin
373 Guinea Field Moor	438 Little Goben	498 Cliff Field	546 Cairn Mellin
374 Lower Field Moor	439 Cugga	499 Park Cairn	549 Park Braaze
375 Inside Bolidden	440 Vental Hill	502 Park Dray	550 Lower Parkenbouggey
376 Homer Bolidden	441 Morrop	503 County Hale	
377 Outer Bolidden	442 Canalier Croft	504 Pen Beagle	552 Park Bougey
378 Great Park Dray	443 Acey Veryan	505 Dunvas	555 Pergollas
379 Dorene	444 Morrop	506 Eleveryan	556 Park Beard
380 Homer Erra	445 Creat Dunvas	507 Round Hill	557 Per Core
381 Outer Erra	446 Little Dunvas	508 Ousher Cliff	558 Per Minor
382 Der Rabbit	447 Per Cere	509 Meadow	561 Park Pound

46 THE LIZARD IN LANDEWEDNACK ~

562 Toulson	617 Pistole Meadow	664 Parkin Ponds	706 Porthpair Field
563 Lower Toulson	619 Trethvas Lane Field	665 Great Park Bew	707 Higher Cairnnithin
565 Meadow	620 Miller	666 Little Park Bew	708 Lower Cairnnithin
567 Downs Field	621 Carrick Widden Garden	667 Great Arraview	709 Lower Derspale
568 Great Telvin		668 Little Arraview	710 Higher Derspale
569 Outer Telvin	622 Canalier Croft	669 Lower Tregoon	711 Whitegate Field
570 Homer Telvin	623 Canalier Garden	670 Higher Tregoon	712 Square Field
571 Moor	624 Chevy Chase	671 Hendy's Higher Field	713 Park Garrack
572 Miller	627 Eira		714 Lighthouse Field
578 Pedingotholan	628 Higher Ver Vere	672 Hendy's Lower Field	715 Indy's Field
579 Canalier	629 Lower Ver Vere		716 Lower Porthpier Field
580 Green Field	630 Pen Beagle	673 Park Broase	
583 Homer Cairnmellin	631 Voslar	674 Parkin Ponds	717 Cellar Field
584 Middle Cairnmellin	632 Eggot	675 Meadow	718 Bolinda
585 Rab Pit Cairnmellin	633 Green Field	673 Park Broase	719 Tidgevean
	634 Trethvas Lane Field	674 Parkin Ponds	720 Lower Houzall
586 Little Cairnmellin		675 Meadow	721 Higher Houzall
587 Cairnmellin Croft	635 Miller	676 Great Telvin	722 Great Houzall
588 Great Canalier	636 Long Croft	677 Outer Telvin	723 Houzall Hill
589 Little Canalier	637 Higher Croft	678 Park Todden	724 Jackys Vortal
590 Higher Park Broaze	638 Orchard Croft	679 Park Noweth	725 Barnets Vortal
591 Parkin Castol	640 Green Field	680 Carrugoon	726 Rellenvellin Hill
592 Garden	642 Per Todden	681 Telvin	727 Higher Menervra
593 Carrick Widden	643 Perkithen	682 Lyne's Lower Field	728 Lower Menervra
594 Homer Park Broase	644 Inside Park Dray	683 Lyne.s Higher Field	729 Homer Terhernot
595 Green Field	645 Outside Park Dray	684 Lyne's Outer Field	730 Lower Terhernot
596 Trethvas Lane Field	646 Great Field	685 Lyne's Mile End Field	731 Higher Terhernot
	647 Dray Field		732 Homer Errathew
597 Miller	648 Clay Pit Field	686 Lizard Downs	733 Outer Errathew
603 Higher Water Field	649 Meadow	689 Erra	734 Ventmeans
604 Lower Water Field	650 Cairngoon Field	690 Ververe	735 Outer Ventmeans
605 Long Meadow	651 Turners Wastrel	691 Carrack Widden	736 Lower Telvin
606 Calves Cliff	652 Old Straw Field	692 Derporter	737 Higher Telvin
607 Carrick Widden	653 Fallow Cairne	693 Errathew	738 Long Telvin
608 Park Tobna	654 Great Cairn	694 Sewarthen	739 Little Field
609 Long Field	655 Cairn Cliff	695 Sewarthen Croft	740 Lower Long Croft
610 Park Mistress	656 Robin Field	696 Cross Widden	741 Higher Long Croft
611 Great Cligger	657 Trethvas Lane	697 Green Field	742 Orchard Croft
612 Little Park Bougey	658 Cairn Goon	698 Lane End	743 Little Cairn Glaze
613 Pistole Cliff	659 Horse Pool	699 Miller	744 Lower Cairn Glaze
614 Kilkanker Field	660 Telvin	702 Jacky's Arra	745 Higher Cairn Glaze
615 Kilkanker Morrop	661 Lower Telvin	703 Barnets Erra	746 Homer Cairngoon
616 Pistole Furze Garden	662 Higher Telvin	704 Inistlegwond	747 Outer Cairngood
	663 Farther Telvin	705 Bolliden	748 Morrop

~ FLOWERING PLANTS ~

The Lizard is famous among botanists for the rare and varied flora, many of which require dedication to find. The visitors walking the cliffs will see many 'pretty' flowers with which they may not be familiar. Owing to the mild climate flowers do not appear at the 'right' time. For example, in November 1995 primroses and violets could be found. Red Campion can usually be found blooming all the year round. The Lesser Celandine, the number of petals of which can vary considerably, may flower during December, but is listed as March to May. Gorse will be found somewhere all the year round, hence the saying, 'Kissing is in season so long as the gorse is blooming'.

The following rough guide is what to expect throughout the year beginning JANUARY-MARCH: Winter Heliotrope, pale lilac, scented flowers with largish auricular leaves; Blackthorn, white flowers before the leaves appear, gives us sloes to harvest; Ivy leaved Toadflax, lilac and yellow small antirrhinum-like flowers on trailing shoots; tall pale yellow flowered, coarse leaved Alexanders in hedgerows; later creamy white Cow Parsley.

These are followed in APRIL by Dandelions; Bulbous Buttercups; Lords and Ladies (Wild Arum) or 'Jack in the Pulpit', large glossy leaves appear in January but flowers in April, has red berries in spikes later which may be hidden by other vegetation; Three- Cornered Leeks (Garlic) which have an unpleasant smell and are often mistaken for white bluebells; Bluebells; Herb Robert (pink); Broom; Sheeps Sorrel, daintier than common sorrel . All these are plentiful. The Spring Squill blooms until June, usually blue, it may be white or pink. Pink Thrift in large cushions. In MAY Borage, blue flowers and cucumber flavoured leaves; pink Sand Wort on serpentine; Chives; Heath Pearlwort, starry white flowers; Oxeye Daisy; Birdsfoot Trefoil, yellow or orange flowers; Rosy Garlic; Spanish Harebell (sturdier than Cornish bluebell); Red valerian (may also be pink or white); Powderblue Sheeps Bit Scabious; Pennywort; Honeysuckle; Foxgloves; Bladder Campion, sweet scented white flowers all add to the glory of the countryside.

In JUNE White Sedum may be found on walls; yellow Ragwort, harmful to cattle, beloved of Cinnabar moth; Teazel with spiny purple heads; yellow St. John's Wort, Thyme, Eyebright (purple lines on yellow); Centuary (pink); Lesser Meadow Rue (purple tinged yellow flowers); Dropwort (creamy white tinged with pink); Greater Burnet (oval heads of dark reddish flowers; pale pink and heath Spotted Orchids; Cross leaved Heath (pink); Bell Heather (crimson purple). The beautiful Burnet Rose grows at Kynance, low growing with purple hips; also the Bloody Cranesbill with large crimson flowers; Yellow

'Erica vagans' (Cornish heath) on the cliffs at Kynance ~

Samphire. On hedges grows yellow Ladies Bedstraw; Yarrow, with flat heads; Wild Carrot (pink buds and white flowers); Rest-harrow (pink pea flowers); Bears Breeches, robust plant with spikes of large white, purple veined flowers; feathery foliaged Tamarisk, with sprays of pink flowers.

In JULY appear the deep purple Ling and Cornish Heath (white, pink or deep lilac) ; Devil's Bit Scabious (light blue). The short straw coloured bracts of Carline Thistle will persist all winter. In AUGUST the silvery leaved Mugwort blooms. In SEPTEMBER the Sea Aster is still blooming as also is the stout woody 3-8 foot Tree Mallow; Butcher's Broom, coarse evergreen plant with beautiful scarlet berries which often remain on the flattened branches throughout the year and is often used for indoor decoration. Hottentot Fig, a South African plant, established on the cliffs, large magenta, pink or pale yellow daisy-like flowers, thick fleshy leaves, tumbles over cliffs and smothers the natural vegetation, leaves turn red in autumn.

These are some of the many flowering plants to be found by the visitor walking the footpaths of this unique botanical area. *Joan Yorston*

EXTRACTS FROM THE DIARY OF MY GREAT GRANDFATHER

~ THOMAS HENDY OF TREGOMINION FARM ~
(in the original spelling)
1859-1887

1859	Jessie Mare fould
1873	Had hiefer calf from J.Hocking

~ 1874 ~

May 4	Wreck of the Night Templor at the Stags laiden with wheat from San Francisco
May 29	Mangolds put in
Oct 2	Mrs confined with a girl
Oct 11	Caught 40 hhds Pilchards Lizard Cove (hhds = hogsheads = 50 gallons)
Oct 30	Caught 30 hhds Pilchards Lizard Cove Thrashed 30 bushels Barley from Mowhay at Brickyard (Brickyard now Brick Cottage)
Nov 13	Carried Mangolds
Nov 19	Tilled wheat in Croft (now Croft Park)
Dec 2	Elie Clift drowned by the upsetting of a boat at Cadgwith

~ 1875 ~

Jan 26	Caen of Cardiff (Steamer) run ashore in a fog at Greenlane
Feb 11	A public Vesting held to revise rating of the parish. Tregominion's rate reduced one pound for the land taken away at the Beacon Four Houses
Feb 19	Front garden (Tregominion) Till to Potatoes
Feb 20	Bought a hiefer calf of Rev. P.V Robinson Colour red and white price 20/-
Mar 5	Tilled onions at Beacon
Mar 27	Lifeboat to sea for practice Carried two loads gravel to Lighthouse for alterations and foghorn

CHAPTER TWO ~ THE LAND

Mar 29 Men commenced work at Lighthouse
Mar 30 Rocket apparatus practice

~ 1876 ~

Jan 26 Had meneage thrashing machine
Feb 19 To Falmouth for a ton of Bone Manure which I bought at auction for £3-4-0
June 17 William came home from Australia Landed at Falmouth, left again on July 28 sailed from Plymouth in the same ship. (William, Thomas and Edgar Hendy migrated to Australia during the Gold Rush days. Thomas returned home after one year and his descendants are still living here. Edgar after a few years moved to America. William stayed in Australia and there are 70 of his descendants still living in the same area).
July 29 Commenced Harvest
Nov 9 Bought two cows for £22-10-0
Nov 10 Solomon Rowe came to live at farm for 16th year
Dec 28 Helston Banking Company Broke

~ 1877 ~

Feb 22 Steam thrashing machine at the farm
Apr 23 Sold the Close Carriage to W.Curtis of Camborne £22-10-0
May 24 The Kimberley Park opened at Falmouth and the St Ives railway opened on the same day
Sept 6 Bazar and fete held in aid of Reading and Lecture Room
Oct 12 Change of weather after 4 weeks dry this has been a wet summer and a wet harvest
Nov 20 Lord Roberts Court at Star Hotel Helston
Dec 28 Sold Mr Dawe Lower Town 12 bushells Barley 12/- per bushell

~ 1878 ~

Jan 20 Fog horn working first time in fog
Feb 23 The hedge to build to fence Reading Room 2/- per day (3/- for horse and cart). Took fifty loads of stone from Grookel Quarry at 1/7½ per load
Mar 20 Steam ship Strombole stuck on Maenheere Rock, afterwards was run into cove and became a total wreck, 16 passengers and a general cargo. Hugh Hocking and myself put the sailors to Falmouth, 20 with two wagons, we had £2-0-0 each.
Mar 29 Electric light first lighted in The Lizard lighthouse
Aug 1 Reading Room open for Subscribers
Sept 4 Rocket apparatus practiced
Sept 17 Reading Room and Lecture Room formally opened by Bickford-Smith of Trevarno and Howard Fox of Falmouth. Freemasons Oddfellows and Foresters formed procession and walked to Church Service. Tea and Concert in the evening.
Dec 17 Sold fat hiefer to Butcher Hendy
Dec 25 Weather broke up after about three weeks of cold with frost. The coldest weather in Cornwall for 20 years.

CHAPTER TWO ~ THE LAND

~ 1879 ~

Mar 4	Oddfellows Lodge opened at Hills Hotel
May 16	Tilled barley in Parc-hithen (now Parc-an-Ithan)
May 24	Lifeboat bell rung by some person unknown, boat to sea not any wreck.
May 29	Drove the Inspector of lifeboats from Cadgwith to St.Keverne 9/- from Cadgwith to Mullion 5/-
June 2	Mullion to Portleven 10/-
July 24	Fetched from Helford pair horses 18/- put them to Mudon Bean Mawnan Smith Life boat crew was paid £8-15-0 assistance to the Brig (Scotch Crag) helpers to have 6/- per man
Oct 16	Clock fixed in Reading Room cost £3-10-0
Dec 15	Caught Pilchards at Cadgwith and The Lizard, a bay boat went down off Green Lane laden with fish crew saved.

~ 1880 ~

Feb 2	Bought bull calf 14/-
May 4	Bought winnowing machine at sale at Cadgwith Farm on the hill £5-6-0
Sept 16	Carried 7 load clay and 3 load clay
Sept 17	Carried 4 load clay and 2 load sand from Polpeor
Sept 18	Carried 6 load stones downs
Oct 1	300 Brick from Gweek 4 loads marl 6 load clay one load sand Kennack
Oct 7	Two wagons to Treath (Helford) for cable for Spanish Company (The cable was laid from Lloyds Signal Station via Housel Bay Beach to Spain)
Oct 8	To Helston with John Lugg to meet Barister to revise votes list. No person rated below £12 a year to be on list, and no person to be on either list no more than once. no dead person to be on list. The charge to meet Barister 11/-
Oct 11	A Committee Meeting held, the balance sheet showed the Reading Room to be out of dept and 30/- in hand
Dec 3	Finished carting earth from Downs to fill pit behind Rocket House 100 loads

~ 1881 ~

April 8	Cencus taken in England
May 10	Paid men for labour in making the garden behind Rocket House £10-13-0
May 31	His Royal Highness the Duke of Edinburgh at The Lizard inspecting Coastguard Houses accompanied with his private sec and inspecting Comander of Falmouth
Aug 3	Weslyan Bazar held in Reading room receiped over £40
Aug 24	New school master Mr. Sealey salary £60-0-0 and half the grant
Nov 18	Waggon and 3 horses from Cadgwith to Penzance with cured Pilchards
Dec 20	Susan Thomas married Ren Triggs

~ 1882 ~

Jan 1	Salvation Army held Three open air services in Weslyan Chapel
Jan 2	The U F Church Methodist had a Xmas tree in Reading Room, proceed for their chapel

~ THE LIZARD IN LANDEWEDNACK 51

April 17	Wm Hendy's wife of Australia died (sister-in-law)
July 6	First Lizard Regatta
Aug 5	To Penzance stopped until 7th then came home in the S.S.Lady of the Isles
Sept 23	Commenced carting stone for Mr. Roberts Falmouth for the two new houses at the station
Nov 14	A man picked up at Housel cove with his head gone was put in the lifeboat house.
Nov 17	A Inquest held on the same man, it proved to be a man from Mousehole which have been missing since 27 Oct

~ 1883 ~

Mar 27-8	Removing Mr. Broad's furniture from Beast Point cottage to Ruan Major (3 loads) 30/- for the work
April 1	Lloyds Company first signal today at The Lizard Signal Station.
April 9	Edgar to Helston School Weslyn, lodging with the master Mr. Hall to pay 4/- per week for his dinners (Edgar's son went to America where five of his six children, all in their 80s, are still living).
April 13	Sold 125 shieves of Reed at 6d a shieve
April 28	Bought 9 Bushels Oats 9 Maize from Collings of Gweek
April 29	Dear Father died after confined to his bed six week and five days with a bad foot and the last two weeks congestion of the lungs, his end was peace age 78 years. Buried 3 May by the side of Mother.
June 23	Found 8 Bullocks at Breage pound after lost them from the Downs, paid 12/- to Mr Richards who kept the pound. Cryer 1/- damage 1/-
July 12	Parson Vivian came to St. Ruan to live. Grand reception given, arches erected, a public tea and procession
Aug 1	Parcel Post come into operation
Aug 9	Commenced harvest by cutting oats in Higher Corfean
Sept 20	Finished carrying corn. Harvest Festival

~ 1884 ~

Jan 14	The School Board elected
Jan 17	Bought a double set of Harness at Parson Bloxams sale Mawgan £4-4-0
Apl 24	Lord Roberts Court
July 4	Wagonette and pair to Falmouth with our own party had a trip up Truro River and came down by train
July 9	Carried hay
Aug 12	6 Bulloacks to Mr Hancocks Kynance
Sept 29	T.H.Hocking left Trenoweth Farm The Lizard and gone to Treganina Budock
Oct 3	Wm Harris left The Lizard and gone to Illogan I removed his goods for £3-0-0
Oct 6	Caught a Badger in Park Ebyer sold it to Mr Keene for 10/-
Oct 25	Finished carting for the Road leading to the Signal Station. Paid Wm Hancock for keeping bullock to grass 30/- Finished repairing Polpeor road and cove more than £200 spent

Dec 22	Sold 1 ton straw to the Farmer at Halfway House
Feb 16	Jno Gilbert left my service having lived with me 9mts 18 days. Sold Rev P V Robinson a pig 23/-
Sept 25	James A Hill sent 9 Bullocks to Erisey pound for straying in his croft at Carnagoon 6 was mine 6 Wm Mitchell
Sept 29	J. Richards went to Gwills Farm Cury to live
Dec 3	At a General Election of the Division of Truro and Helston was contested by Wm Bickford Smith ~ No of Votes 3816 and Wm Molsworth St Aubyn ~ No of Votes 2883 = Majority ~ 933

~ 1886 ~

Mar 20	SS... of Venice came ashore at Penvose Cadgwith Lifeboat went to Falmouth with her they were paid £60 (the Rocket went to her but was not wanted I charged 20/- by night
Mar 22	The Barque Sidnham came to anchor at the Rill, was taken to Falmouth by the tug, the Rocket went almost to Kynance but was not wanted
May 5	Hugh Lyne died at Penzance age 35
Sept 28	SS Suffolk came ashore at Lizard Head and became a total wreck, coming from Baltimore bound for London laiden with Flour, Walnut timber, Tin Oysters, Tomatoes and 163 Bullocks !
Oct 6	Bought 31 Bags of flour salved from the wreck at Housel at 2/9 a bag
Oct 19	Bought Headstone and Curb from Mr Pascoe of Penzance and put them in memory of Father and Mother, Paid £9-0-0 for it
Nov 4	Getting stones to carry on high roads I took pile to Trethvas Gate and inside Directing Post, I took some to Lizard Town 1/10 a load
Nov 5	To Camborne with 3 horses and waggon for Rich Brays goods as agreed to work with me three day a week for 6/- and a house to live in and to till a bushell of potatoes
Dec 9	Bought pair of spectikles of Mr Myers of Plymouth for Edgar paid 7/6 towards 10/- which he charged for them, then another 2/6 when he came again and a chance to change them for another pair.

~ 1887 ~

Jan 7	Four carts carting rub from Rean to J Goodmans Smith Shop 35 yards at 1/10 30 load and 6 loads not measured
Feb 22	Had steam thrashing machine
Feb 26	Tilled potatoes in Front Garden
Mar 13	Wreck of the Gypsey Queen (schooner) of Padstow on Maenheere Rock laden with cement
May 5	Paid C J Richards for his two colts up the 1 May, the Mare to be kept from May 1 for 1/6 a week Tilled Mangolds

Thomas Hendy was born 1839, died 1924 aged 85

CHAPTER TWO ~ THE LAND

The Family Tree of the Diarist ~ Thomas Hendy
(1839 ~ 1924)
of Tregoninion Farm, The Lizard

Thomas S. Hendy = Sally
born 1805 ~ died 1883 / died 1853

Children: Caroline; Thomas (born 1839, died 1924) = Loveday; Edgar

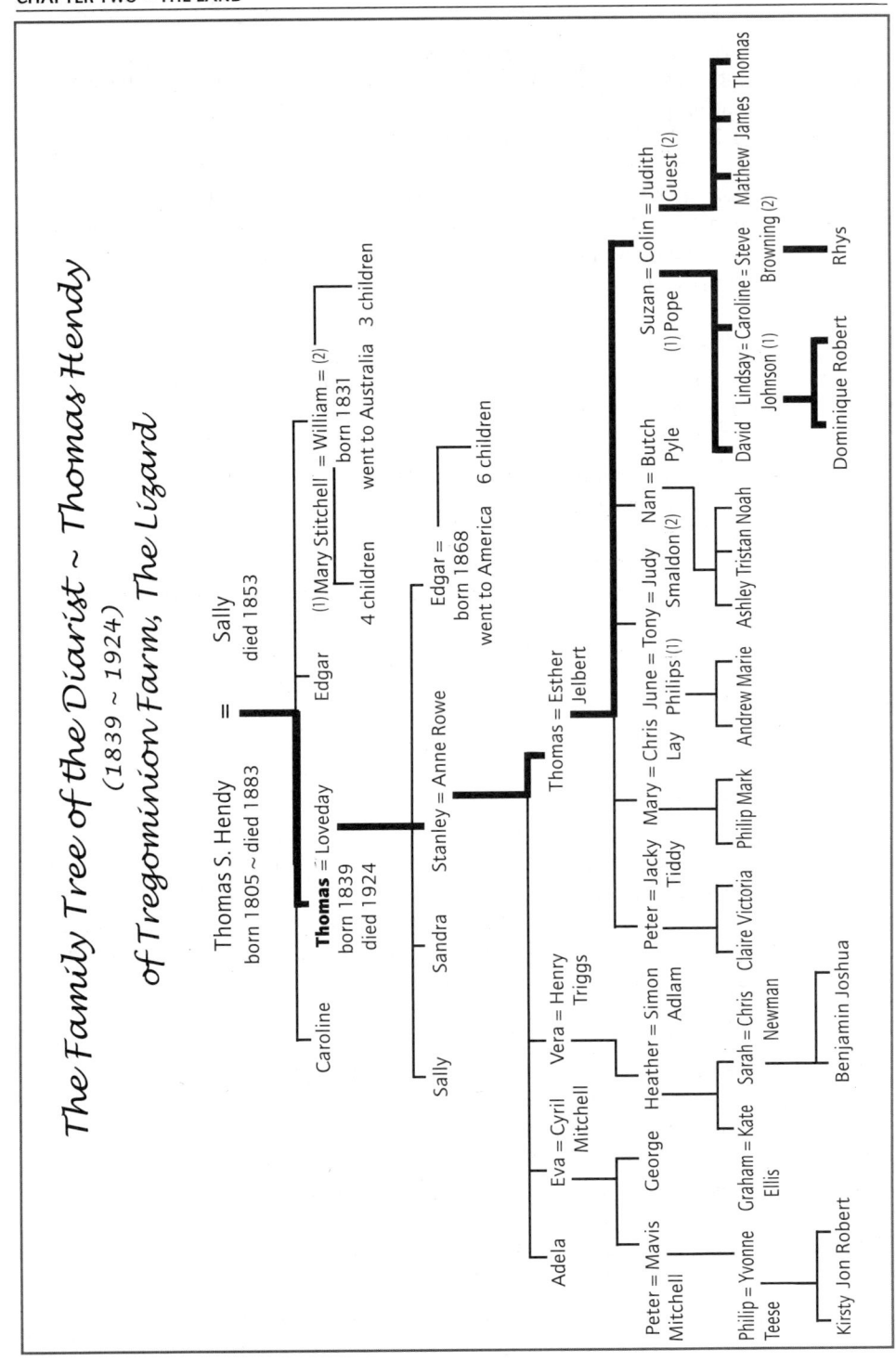

Thomas = Loveday branch:
- Sally
- Sandra
- Stanley = Anne Rowe
- Thomas = Esther Jelbert

Edgar branch:
- Mary Stitchell (1) = William (born 1831, went to Australia, 3 children) = (2) [4 children]
- Edgar (born 1868, went to America, 6 children)

Thomas = Esther Jelbert children and descendants:

Adela

Peter = Mavis Mitchell
- Philip = Yvonne Teese
  - Kirsty, Jon, Robert

Eva = Cyril Mitchell
- George
- Graham = Kate Ellis
  - Benjamin, Joshua

Vera = Henry Triggs
- Heather = Simon Adlam
- Sarah = Chris Newman

Peter = Jacky Tiddy
- Claire Victoria

Mary = Chris Lay
- Philip Mark

June = Tony Philips (1)
- Andrew Marie

Judy Smaldon (2)

Nan = Butch Pyle
- Ashley Tristan Noah

Suzan = Colin = Judith Guest (2)
Pope (1)
- Mathew James Thomas

David

Lindsay = Caroline = Steve Browning (2)
Johnson (1)
- Dominique Robert
- Rhys

54   THE LIZARD IN LANDEWEDNACK ~

~ HOUSEL BAY HOTEL 1894-1994 ~

Imagine the scene. Just over 100 years ago a small group of men stand on the cliffs close to Lizard Point, top hats silhouetted against the bright sky, frock coats fluttering in the light breeze. They gaze down at the Atlantic waves crashing on the rocks below. Agreement is reached, a decision made. This will be the perfect place for a new hotel.

Tourism was just beginning in Cornwall. The first tourists were rich people and a number of hotels were under construction around the coast to accommodate discerning guests. The group of local business men, meeting on the cliff top that day, planned to benefit from these wealthy visitors and commissioned a well known local architect, Silvanus Trevail, to design the new hotel. Plans were laid, designs approved. The hotel, as the original builder said, was 'positively carved out of the rock ~ for the stone with which it was built came from the hill on which it stood and was carved and formed upon the spot'.

The hotel was officially opened in June 1894. One of those present, local farmer Thomas Hendy, wrote in his diary: 'Housel Bay Hotel opened by the shareholders with a cold luncheon. About 40 sat down to a very good spread'. The West Briton reported on the occasion: 'To celebrate the opening a large company were entertained by the Directors in the dining room'.

Some of the early days of the hotel are mentioned in a diary kept by Frances Jenkin who lived in Lizard village and whose father and uncle were both shareholders in the hotel. At the beginning of August 1894 she reports seeing twenty ships of the fleet going down channel and that the same week 'Races were held in the village. The Lizard is full of trippers of a very second rate description. There was a concert in the Housel Bay reading room in the evening'. The diary also comments on the first dissatisfied guest : 'On August 12 Captain George left the hotel in a huff after threatening to fight Mr. Ayres and shoot himself because the former disturbed him the night before by walking about above him'. In October Miss Jenkins describes how one day she 'sheltered from the rain in Housel Bay Hotel' and as the wind increased to gale force sat in the drawing room and watched the sea while the glass in the windows bent in the storm. A letter from her aunt in Plymouth about this time expressed the hope that the hotel would 'answer the most sanguine expectations of the shareholders. It will be a fresh source of interest [for you] to watch the arrivals and departures, and if it brings more of the upper ten your mother will be in her element...perhaps I shall find my nephews and nieces marrying lords and ladies...'

Notable guests did stay at the hotel and some of the registers read like a Who's Who of the period. In 1898 Henry Wood came to stay and in 1900 Marconi and his wife. In that year also the wife and daughter of Benjamin Disraeli spent a fortnight at the hotel. Baroness Von Richthofen came in 1904 ~ she was the wife of the famous Red Baron, the German flying ace of the First World War ~ and in 1908 royalty were visitors when the then Prince of Wales, later George V, arrived with his wife. In the years which followed, bishops and archbishops, dukes, admirals, generals and members of high society were among the guests. So too were writers, painters, politicians and other public figures, including George Bernard Shaw, Sidney and Beatrice Webb, W.H. Auden and Augustus John, Douglas Bader, G.K. Chesterton and Kenneth Grahame.

In 1930 there was a dramatic cliff rescue near Housel Bay when one of the hotel guests, a Miss Johnson, slipped and fell down a cliff. She was caught on a ledge for some hours while villagers and hotel staff tried to rescue her. Eventually she was helped to safety, unharmed. A diary entry by one of the guests at the time comments: 'Many of the local villagers were standing on the beach below watching the rescue. As the young lady was pulled to safety a collective sigh went up from the assembled people. It may have been relief that she was finally safe but I suspect a secondary factor was that many of those below had an interesting view of the lady's petticoats!'

In the early 1940's Housel Bay was used as a billet for army and later for RAF personnel. In 1943 it was occupied by a Women's Auxiliary Air Force Radar Plotting team. The station was commanded by Flying Officer William Croft who started an affair with one of the WAAFs, Joan Lewis. When the affair became common knowledge senior officers stepped in and arranged for Joan to be transferred to Devon. Before this could happen, in the early hours of the morning of 16 October 1943 a shot was heard coming from the summer house in the hotel gardens. Then a second shot and Croft was seen leaving the summer house. From there he went to the duty officer and said he had shot Joan. She was found shot twice, once through the heart. At his trial Croft claimed that there had been a suicide pact which went wrong. He said that after shooting Joan he had tried to kill himself but that the gun failed to fire on the third occasion. The jury rejected his evidence and he was convicted of murder. Although sentenced to death, his sentence was commuted to life imprisonment .

It was rumoured afterwards that the ghost of a young woman was sometimes to be seen in the hotel gardens. In October 1978 a guest at the hotel, who was a practising medium, claimed to have seen and spoken to the girl, who said she was waiting in the gardens for her lover to join her as he had promised when they made their pact in 1943. A year later in August 1979 an artist staying at the hotel told the proprietor that he had been so surprised to see a young woman dressed in RAF uniform sitting in the gardens looking out to sea that he had made a drawing of her.

One afternoon in March 1973 the hotel was badly damaged by fire. Two ladies who were walking the coastal path came in for a cream tea and sat in the lounge. Both were smokers and on their departure one of them left a cigarette smouldering in the ash tray. A gust of wind must have blown the curtains against it and the hotel's owners returned from an afternoon walk to see the lounge ablaze and fire threatening to engulf the first floor bedrooms above . Fortunately most of the guests were out, and the others, along with the owners' children were safely evacuated through a rear exit. The Fire Brigade was quickly on the scene. One local fireman spent the entire time playing his hose on the wall between the lounge and the bar despite efforts to get him to turn his attention to hosing down one of the bedrooms . As he said, ' If the fire spreads to the bar with its thatched roof and inflammable alcohol , then there would be no chance of saving the hotel', adding, 'If we don't keep the fire from spreading to the bar, I won't get my pint tomorrow!' . Although the lounge and two bedrooms above were severely damaged, the rest of the hotel was saved. There was though a great deal of mess everywhere from the water and the smoke and it looked as if it might be several months before the hotel could be reopened . As the owners surveyed the scene next day they looked up and saw, coming down the lane to the hotel, a stream of villagers. Most of these were women wearing headscarves and carrying mops and buckets. Almost every woman in the village turned out that morning to help clean up the hotel. It was open again only six weeks later.

The Housel Bay has, in just a hundred years , had a fascinating and chequered history, and there seems little doubt that the next hundred years will be just as interesting and colourful.

~ THE MOST SOUTHERLY POST OFFICE ~

I was Post Master at The Lizard Post Office for 36 years prior to my retirement in 1973. The original Post Office was situated in Kynance Terrace but in 1897 my grandfather Richard Tiddy built a new Post Office in the village. A newspaper report states that Richard's daughter, Clara, laid the foundation stone and the local band played during the ceremony. My father, Richard Henry Tiddy, was the first Sub-Postmaster to take charge of the new office and held the position for some 38 years after which I took over and on my retirement my son Mike ran the business until 1988. In my father's time mail was brought from Helston by pony and trap and parcels were packed into large wicker crates for easy transportation. The mail was sorted here and delivered on foot to outlying areas. The Post Office clock was the main timepiece in the village and in the days before radio or television people would set their watches by it before going off to work.

In 1903 the GWR introduced the first omnibus service in the country. It ran between Helston and The Lizard and our mail was despatched by it. On 17 August 1978 a special First Day Cover was issued from our Post Office to commemorate the 75th anniversary of this bus service.

Morse code was the main means of communication in the early 1900s and my father was an expert telegrapher. When the White Star liner *'Suevic'* went aground on Maenheere Rock off The Lizard in 1907 lifeboats went to her assistance and all the passengers were rescued. The survivors came to the Post Office to send messages home to Australia. Two extra operators had to be brought from Falmouth to deal with the rush of work. When the Telephone Exchange was introduced in 1932 that too was kept busy dealing with emergency messages. Our exchange covered The Lizard, Cadgwith, Ruan and Kuggar as well as eight coastguard stations. When bad weather watch was in operation the Postmaster had little rest as the exchange was in operation almost continually and he had to man it at all times.

We had almost 100 evacuees in the village during the war, mostly from the Tottenham area and every time the mail arrived they would rush to the Post Office hoping for a letter from home. Often they were disappointed and it used to break my heart to tell them there was no letter for them. Most of the parents were very concerned about their children, but there were some who rarely received a letter from home.

The 400th anniversary of the Armada celebrations was commemorated by a First Day Cover issued from the Post Office here and requests were received for it from

Post Office and G.W.R. Parcels receiving office (left) about 1907 ~

photo J. Hart

CHAPTER TWO ~ THE LAND

all over the world. It was a mammoth task to hand frank these Covers with The Lizard date stamp. This was the final task performed by the Tiddy family after nine decades as Postmasters. It was the end of an era.

Postmasters at The Lizard:

1856	William Lawrence
1873	Henry Hendy
1883/9	Thomas Stirling
1897	Richard Henry Tiddy (new Post Office)
1937	Douglas Tiddy
1973	Mike Tiddy
1988	Leonard Trott

The village pump outside the Post Office, and Oliver's Temperance House on the right ~

photo J. Hart

Douglas Tiddy

~ THE CHAPEL ~

At The Lizard by the 1850s a small Wesleyan chapel had been built on Cross Common and was well attended; there was no music or hymn books and hymn tunes were pitched by one of the congregation with words drawn from memory. A minister would take the service about four times a year, but on other Sundays a local preacher would undertake the duty, or, if he failed to turn up, a prayer meeting would be held by those present.

There came a time when it was decided that a bigger chapel was needed and so the present chapel in Housel Bay Road was built in 1864 from local stone, quarried and transported free of charge by local farmers. The chapel on Cross Common was sold and converted into a house. At about this time a breakaway group built a separate chapel on the Village Green and over the following years both chapels flourished with up to 200 worshippers at the Wesleyan Chapel in Housel Bay Road and 75 at the United Methodist Free Church known as the 'Little Ship' on the Village Green. At the Wesleyan Chapel the choir alone at one time numbered 20. As the twentieth century proceeded, the desire to attend chapel diminished and by 1935 the two chapels decided to combine the forces of their reduced membership. They accordingly amalgamated into the now-named Wesleyan Methodist Chapel in Housel Bay Road. The chapel on the Village Green was then sold and became a private residence which is still there.

In 1880 the present chapel was extended by the addition of a large room for the Sunday School and while this was being built services were held for a time in the recently constructed

Reading Room. The fund-raising activities connected with the building of this extension included a bazaar which raised £20 ~ more than the yearly average wage. At Christmas 1891 the Wesleyans had a Christmas tree and tea and refreshments ~ and the United Free Church did the same a few days later in the New Year. Until the installation of a new pipe organ in 1895 the music was provided by a pedal harmonium. Before the days of the motor car the minister's horse or pony and trap was left across the way at Mr. Hendy's farm. Over the years other improvements were made to the chapel. Petrol vapour lights provided in 1912 were replaced by electric lights in the 1930s. The latest modification to the building was the addition of the kitchen and modern toilet 1952.

During the storms of 1979, however, the roof of the Sunday Schoolroom was badly damaged. This was replaced with an entirely new roof by a government-sponsored youth group from Redruth at a cost to the chapel of just the materials. The Lizard Youth Club went on a sponsored walk to help the project and raised the magnificent sum of £462. Further funds of nearly £300 were received from other parts of the country following a notice in the Methodist Gazette.

The chapel now has a woman minister, the Reverend Sylvia Burgoyne, who has responsibility for five other chapels and is based at Mullion. She takes about eight services a year at The Lizard. Other services are led by local preachers of the Helston circuit or even on occasion by members of the congregation. *Courtney Rowe*

~ LIZARD FEAST ~

One of the great occasions of the year was Lizard Feast, held on the Sunday nearest to 19th June. According to 'A Corner of Old Cornwall' (E. Bonham, 1896) there was in the nineteenth century a great deal of activity in the days leading up to the Feast. Houses would be tidied up and whitewashed, for on Feast Saturday friends and relations would arrive and stay for up to a week, the duration of the festivities. Much cooking preparation was necessary, especially of bread, saffron cakes and pasties ~ at Churchtown Farm alone there was enough for 40 people. Feast Sunday was a special day with popular services in the morning followed by a traditional dinner of lamb pie whose ingredients also included parsley and cream. On Feast Monday a couple from Helston would arrive on the Village Green and set up a stall selling saffron buns, bread, nuts, rock and fairings.

In the twentieth century Feast Sunday continued to be a highlight of the village year, especially for the Wesleyan Methodists, marking as it did the anniversary of the opening of the Chapel and the Sunday School. Everyone had a new outfit and the children took part in singing special hymns in the chapel services at 11 a.m., 2.30 p.m. and 6 p.m. The number of stalls on the Village Green gradually increased, extending down to the post office and remaining in operation from Monday to Wednesday. On Feast Monday the children of the Wesleyan Sunday School, headed by a band and carrying banners, would parade through the village. They always stopped at the house of Miss Thomas in Penmenner Road where she gave each child a bag of sweets, and then moved on to visit Miss Wallis at Maenheere. The parade was followed by sports and a free tea for the Sunday School children, with the special treat of a large saffron bun for each child. On Feast Tuesday, until 1935 when it amalgamated with the Wesleyans, the United Free Chapel on the Green held their own procession with a band, and made their way to Penmenner House where the children were given oranges and sweets. Feast Wednesday was 'Church Day', when it was the parish church's turn to celebrate. Mothers and children of the congregation squeezed into farm wagons and trundled to Kennack Sands and a picnic tea with saffron Feast buns .

There is now very little left of Lizard Feast. It has been taken over by the British Legion with a band concert and sports and a tea for the children on the Saturday after the Sunday nearest 19th June. *Courtney Rowe*

~ THE LIZARD READING ROOM ~

J.C. Trewin in his book Up from The Lizard refers to the 'solid little Reading Room at the end of the Beacon'. In September 1878 The Lizard Reading and Lecture Room was formally opened by Mr.W. Bickford Smith of Trevarno and Mr. Howard Fox of Falmouth and other gentlemen. The ceremony was followed by a public tea and a concert in the evening in aid of the Building Fund, which at that time was still £80 short of the £300 needed to cover the cost of the building. Records show that the deficiency was quickly cleared, leaving the villagers with an institution of which they were justly proud.

None of this would have come to pass if it had not been for the friendly relations which existed between the Direct Spanish Cable Company and the Government signalling and clerical staff who were working together as a community at the Lloyds Signal Station. It appears that these men believing that there was a need in the village for a hall large enough to be used for public entertainment set up the committee which raised the necessary funds.

The Reading Room was soon established as the centre of all social activities and in the years which followed many happy evenings were enjoyed by the villagers at dances and concerts. A Library was added, but it soon became clear that room was needed for further recreational activities such as billiards. As result a committee of local people was formed to raise funds to extend the building, and one of the events which they arranged was a quite extraordinary Flower Show. Mr. Bickford Smith, the local member of Parliament, arranged for his head gardener to supervise the show and to provide many rare and expensive plants. Local artists, hearing about the show, loaned some of their pictures; Brock & Sons of Crystal Palace fame lent a quantity of Chinese lanterns to decorate the hall, and the H.M.S. Ganges boy band provided musical items. The show brought in distinguished visitors from all around. Everything combined to make an event the like of which had never been seen in The Lizard before.

J.C. Trewin records another outstanding event in the Reading Room when in May 1913 The Lizard was more excited than it had been since the last Feast Monday sports. The event ~ 'The Pictures had come' ~ and would appear at the Reading Room !! The Room was hastily furnished with benches and a white crinkly sheet hung on the wall. Boys perched themselves on the windowsills, making their usual rackety noise, while parents and young children huddled tightly together on the backless benches waiting for the epic, 'Uncle Tom' to begin. Amid the stuttering light the heroine of the film, Little Eva, was seen upside down and the audience swayed each time the film moved off the screen. Finally, at the end of the show the lantern fell to the floor with a crash and one small boy put his hand through a window ~ but all in all it was a triumphant evening. The pictures had come to The Lizard and box office returns were over one pound.

Such was the enthusiasm of Percy Rendell from Mile End in 1917 that he was able to mobilise the whole village in the production of 'The Geisha'. Amid grave doubts from the older inhabitants, the village took to the stage, and with such success that even the roaring boys who used to whistle and bang from the windowsills of the Reading Room were reduced to silence. In the years between the wars the Reading Room, guided by the Trustees, continued to meet the social needs of the village. Regular dances with a band were held, the most popular musicians at the time being the 'Four Aces' from Penzance, and the high-light of the year being the New Year Dance. Film shows and whist drives also became part of the regular entertainment programme. The Reading Room was also used as the doctor's consulting room until the new surgery was built. Even today the Room is used on a regular basis for appointments with the visiting optician from Helston.

During the 1940s a Mr. and Mrs. James came to live in the village and it was because of their initiative and drive that a fund raising committee was established to raise money to build an extension to the Reading Room. On 15th February 1951 that extension was duly opened by Mrs. Bickford Smith and made provision for a large billiard-snooker room, known as the James Room, later on The Lizard Snooker Club, along with a committee room, the Mrs. James Room, now the Ladies Room, together with new kitchen and toilet facilities.

As the years passed, new organisations found their roots in the Reading Room. In 1951 The Lizard Women's Institute was founded, and in 1961 the Badminton Club saw its beginnings. January 1988 was the occasion of the first Lizard Lights pantomime, 'Cinderella', written and produced by the late Syd Yorston, who continued to write and produce an annual pantomime until 1994. The Armada celebration was perhaps the next landmark among Reading Room events. July 1988 was the 400th anniversary of the sighting of the Spanish Armada off The Lizard. To commemorate this occasion fund-raising events were held in the Reading Room, together with endless 'working parties' ceaselessly making yards and yards of flags and bunting to decorate the village. The celebrations began with a lavish Elizabethan Banquet organised by The Lizard W.I. and finishing with the Elizabethan Ball. Both events will be remembered for the splendour of the costumes and the authentic decor of the hall.

After this there was something of a lull in Reading Room affairs. A Management Committee took over from the Trustees and began again the task of raising funds, this time to replace the floor in the main hall after 113 years of wear and tear, and to install a new central heating system. This was accomplished after two years hard work and with the help of grants gratefully received from the Cornwall County Council, Kerrier District Council, Landewednack Parish Council, H.R.H. the Prince of Wales Fund, the Sports Council, and Lloyds Bank and from countless private donors. And so into the future ~ for much still remains to be done.

Bill Smallbone

~ THE LIZARD PAVILION ~

An alternative venue for social gatherings was successfully provided five years ago when the long established 'Lizard Argyle' football team was instrumental in building 'The Football and Social Club' on the foundations of the old Cadet Hut.

George Carter

~ THE SCHOOL ~

Early days ~ 1884-1901~

In the nineteenth century Landewednack school was originally a 'voluntary' one. Voluntary schools were of two main kinds; 'National', ones owned and run by the Anglican Church, and 'British' ones by Nonconformists. They were called 'voluntary' schools because they were maintained by local voluntary donations and school fees paid by parents.

These schools did not cover all the country and most did not provide much in the way of education. In 1870 an Education Act reorganised elementary education for children up to the age of eleven by ordering local authorities to provide schools, run by School Boards, wherever voluntary schools were inadequate. Some areas struggled on for years with their existing voluntary arrangements before giving up their educational independence and electing a School Board to take over control of the school. This seems to be what happened in Landewednack.

We know very little about the voluntary school, which was a National one, for all its Log Books and attendance registers were 'lost'. when the school was closed at Christmas 1883. Four months later, on Tuesday, 15 April 1884, the school reopened as a Board school in the old premises (now Carn Hyr, opposite the present school). The new Master was not impressed with what he found. He wrote in his first weekly entry in his new Log Book: 'Found the school in a very backward state. The children are noisy and careless'. Closer examination confirmed his first impressions for a week later he wrote 'Several children cannot read easy monosyllables without spelling them out first ... and their writing is most inferior. The discipline is unsteady and the whole school is given to idling and talking. Home Lessons are not well done'. Later he wrote 'The work done (this week) gave the Master satisfaction, but teaching cannot have been easy for him. He taught singlehanded in one room 50 or more children aged between six and eleven divided into four or five Standards or classes. His wife, the Mistress, taught the infants and supervised the girls' needlework. Although the number of children in the school gradually increased, it was several years before the Board was persuaded to engage additional help in the person of an unqualified girl as an assistant teacher.

The most dreaded day in the school year was that of the annual government inspection. Sometime in May the inspector would arrive and examine the children. On the results of the examination, and of satisfactory attendance records, depended the next year's grant and therefore the future of the school and its staff. Year after year the inspector reported lack of educational progress and failures of discipline ~ 'the scholars have not distinguished themselves...and seem to prefer clandestine conversation to diligent application. Discipline is much as it was ~ there are traces of copying and dishonest work'. Every year too there were criticisms about the state of the building ~ 'the dismal inconvenient room in which the infants are confined'...'the premises are as unsatisfactory as ever'... 'the ventilation needs attention ... the girls' Offices are much too public'... and so on.

In 1892 a worse than usual report by the inspector, coupled with the Master's illness and a great increase in the number of students (the government had at last made elementary education not only compulsory but also free) resulted in a clean sweep of existing teachers, and their replacement with trained staff in large enough numbers to deal with the roll of 135 pupils. In effect it was a new beginning for the school, but progress was hampered by obvious overcrowding. Staff complained of the 'close atmosphere of the rooms' and the children's 'packed condition'. Disease spread rapidly and the Log Books are full of references to outbreaks of influenza, whooping cough, and measles and the 'small school' (i.e. low attendance) which resulted. The worst epidemic though was of diphtheria 1892-3, in which a member of staff was seriously affected and one boy died.

Illness was not the only reason for low attendance. The Log Books reveal that pupils stayed away to watch cricket matches, to go blackberrying, and to 'help' with wrecks. A wreck off Polpeor in July 1888 led to 50 per cent absenteeism ~ 'These wrecks injure the school', complained the Master thinking of the bad effect it would have on the attendance grant. In November 1900 there was 'unsatisfactory attendance all week partly owing to the wreck of a Norwegian barque off Polpeor: the bigger boys are wrecking and the smaller ones are busy carrying dinners etc.' Sometimes, though, absence from school was official. Lizard Feast, Queen Victoria's Diamond Jubilee, the Chrysanthemum Show, the Rector wanting the use of the premises, or the election of a new School Board were all legitimate reasons for the school being closed. Occasionally there might be other and unexpected excitements, as in August 1895 when Mr. J. Roberts visited the school and, having lectured the children suitably on their duty to obey and respect their parents, invited them all to tea at his house, Maenheere (now Wartha Manor).

In October 1893 the School Board, forced by increasingly vigorous criticisms in the Inspector's annual report to do something about providing more suitable accommodation, accepted Mr. Tiddy's tender of £663 for building a new school. Until this could be ready the children were moved into temporary premises. It is not certain where this was, but it was probably the Church Sunday School Room. Wherever it was there does not seem to have been overmuch room, for the Log Book is full of complaints about overcrowding and the close, hot and stuffy atmosphere which resulted. On 11 January 1895 the Master was able to write : 'Reopened in our new school on Tuesday last. Will take us a little time to settle down'. It did, for there were teething troubles. The Inspector thought the ventilation inadequate and demanded improvements should be made; the playground was not ready for use until the end of the summer, and desperate attempts to improve its surface during the winter by spreading 'fine earth' over it 'made bad matters worse' when heavy rain turned the whole area initially into a muddy quagmire. These minor problems once overcome, Landewednack School was ready to face the twentieth century.

Andrina Stiles.

~ EXTRACTS FROM THE SCHOOL LOG BOOK 1901-1952 ~

1910-1922

Oct 6 1910	Called attention of the Attendance officer to George Bray's absence from the school on the plea of illness; he was seen in charge of a horse and cart last Friday and has been about the village on several days.
Dec 20 1911	Mr. T. Hendy, one of the Managers, visited the school today. Owing to very heavy rain only 37 children present out of 94. Part of pane of glass was blown out by the wind on Wednesday night ~ this caused much draught in the main room, the registers not being marked in consequence.

Feb 12 1912	Poor attendance throughout week owing to sickness and bad weather. Main schoolroom temperature varied from 41 to 43 F. It was decided to light the fire at 8 am until further notice or until such time as the weather shall improve.
Feb 16 1912	Owing to the report of a barque having come ashore, three boys were wanted at 11 am. Their attendances were cancelled. Several children were absent for this reason on Thursday afternoon.
Nov 1 1912	Launcelot Imber is unable to attend. He has been operated upon at Truro Hospital and is not likely to attend for several weeks.
Feb 7 1913	Small attendance on Tuesday morning (Shrove Tuesday) owing to old local custom 'Colperra'.
Jul 25 1917	Closed school this afternoon on account of the Wesleyan Band of Hope outing to Kennack Sands.
May 27 1918	On account of her marriage Miss Ellis (infants' teacher) has been granted leave of absence for two days.
Feb 28 1922	School closed in honour of the wedding of Princess Mary and Viscount Lascelles.

The Second World War and After

Sep 11 1939	Last week school closed owing to outbreak of War. 100% of children complete with Respirators were present this morning.
Jun 20 1940	During this week we have received 67 evacuees from London. They arrived on Monday, being received at the school. In normal circumstances the school would be closed for Lizard Feast but owing to the exceptional situation the school has remained open. Attendance of locals exceedingly good.
Jun 24 1940	We have received instructions that our school and the evacuated school in the Reading Room shall work alternately, our school working a $3^{1}/_{2}$ hour session this week and a 3 hour session next week ~ this until further notice.
Aug 22 1940	A wireless receiving set has been obtained for children to hear the up-to-date war news.
Sep 1 1940	Tottenham children are merging with ours and numbers on our books are now as follows: Locals 77~ Bristol 58 ~ L.C.C. 38 ~ Plymouth 18 ~ Others 27 = Total 218
Jun 28 1945	Numbers down to 99 children. Only 7 evacuees left. We have ceased using the Reading Room as a school.
Oct 8 1951	Mrs Imber of 11 Beacon Terrace reports she has heard someone moving about in the playground on two successive nights, once at about 3 am. The intruder seems to be shovelling coke which lies about in piles. I have complained about this matter several times. Mrs Eva Mitchell of Kynance Bay Private Hotel reported that she had a basket containing a tin of beef stolen from her bike in the Girl's playground between 7.30 and 9 p.m., this whilst attending a meeting at the school.
Feb 6 1952	Today Class 1 had just completed a map of Princess Elizabeth's tour of Kenya, Ceylon and Australia when I turned on the wireless for the Current Affairs programme, only to hear the announcement of the King's sudden death. The class stood for a minute in silence.

Jul 24 1952 A fire inadvertently occurred in the coke-house after lunch break today. Four senior boys ~ Green 15, Imber 14, Olivey 14 and Pitman 13 had been instructed to burn some paper in a dustbin ~ this being situated some 12' to 15' from the open coke-house door, inside being stacked with old timber and various rubbish. Wind due east ~ very fresh breeze. Some 20 minutes after Assembly had commenced I was alerted to the fact that smoke was seen to be issuing from the coke-house, a passerby having raised the alarm. The Fire Brigade was called as all the salvage was alight, but after 15 minutes, with the aid of a stirrup pump the blaze was brought under control.
The jumble sale due to start at 3 p.m. suffered somewhat from the distraction of the fire but nevertheless raised £15 for school funds.
101 children on school roll at end of school year.

(Neville Green says that he and his class-mates had well and truly 'stoked' the fire, hoping to be allowed to watch over this instead of attending Assembly ~ unfortunately that was not allowed)
Derry Dobson

~ WARTHA MANOR ~

The story of 'local lad makes good' began for John Roberts when he acquired work in a haberdashery in far away London. Progressing from this relatively humble start he went on to amass considerable wealth by making fashionable ladies veils, on which his first wife then stuck the required number of black chenille spots.

Being a local farmer's son, he returned home to build a house for his growing family ~ Wartha Manor ~ a four-square granite house standing at the top of Penmenner Road. The Architect was the well-known Cornishman Sylvanus Trevail who designed Housel Bay Hotel .

Both John's first and second wives (two sisters) died young and he married once more ~ a charming French lady from Lille, whom he had met whilst involved with the silk trade in France. Madame Roberts is well remembered amongst the older villagers, but she left the village in the early twenties and Ernest, one of the sons, later sold the property to a Mr. Bond who lived there until Mr. and Mrs. Wallis and their daughter Robina bought the house in 1931. Miss Wallis died in 1986, leaving Wartha Manor to the National Trust, the only reminder of its original owner being his initials J.A.R. 1894. carved above the front door. *Derry Dobson*

~ THE LIZARD BRICK AND PIPE WORKS 1851-1867 ~

In the summer of 1848 T.J. Robartes ~ the Honourable Anna Maria Agar's son ~ had asked his landagent Alfred Jenkins what could be done to remedy 'the want of employment for the labouring classes', and the reply was 'I should like to try the experiment 'draining' on a small piece of thy land'. Alfred Jenkin's eldest son, Silvanus W. Jenkin, had been reading about this in a book, and in fact it was later he and his half-brother Pearse Jenkin who were put in charge of The Lizard Brick and Pipe Works.

CHAPTER TWO ~ THE LAND

Extracts from the Records of the Brick and Pipe Works ~

1848   Manor of Predannack, belonging to Robartes, spent £29 on drainage and £209 in the following year.

1848   Five tons of one inch pipes were ordered from Bridgewater, sent to Gweek by sea.

1849   Wet clay land worth only 5/- per acre became worth 20/- per acre (Later two clay pits were to be dug down Signal Lane and some clay was taken from Lizard Downs ~ Robartes' land).

1850   Drainage was described as something of a 'new thing' in these parts '

1851   It has been established that the local brickyard was started on behalf of the Honourable Anna Maria Agar of Lanhydrock under the supervision of Pearse Jenkin, the son of her steward . (It is fairly certain that The Lizard works were in strong competition with the Bridgwater Brick works from the beginning)

1854   Coals sent by sea and landed at Church Cove ~ some being obtained from Llanelly.

1856   The cost of Lizard bricks were then 30/- per thousand.

1857   A vessel brought 53 tons of coal and took away a cargo of brick for Truro.

1859   A vessel from Penzance for serpentine stone was to take in addition 3,000 more 2 inch pipes for Roskennalls.

1859   Cost of carriage to Redruth for 50 to 100 thousand bricks wanted for New Public Rooms (the Druids Hall ~ now a furniture shop) was 25/- a thousand. This year at least 50 copies of a raised price list was given to regular customers. It is also noted that in January of the same year 'no men were to be engaged until S.W. Jenkin had been down and made a new agreement' (did it only function in the Summer months?)

1860   Pearse Jenkin wrote -'I cannot consent to lowering price nor to lessen the number of hands at the yard as we should not then be able to make enough pipes to supply our customers in the winter. It does no more than pay working expenses as it is'. There was also a difficulty in getting some landowners to pay. Prices were going up ~ a 2 inch pipe costing £1.15s. a thousand. Flooring tiles were then being made as well. End of year stock as follows- 16,000 bricks, 1,000 9 inch floor tiles ~ a larger dog being introduced to guard the yard.

1860   Pearse Jenkin wrote 'there must be greater accommodation afforded to visitors against another season'. His Father recommended a house to T.J. Agar Robartes for a stay, referred to as 'our new lodging house,(at Landewednack). It was built and kept by William Jeffery, and called 'Brick House'. (This being opposite the gate into Brick Yard and presumably made wholly from Lizard bricks) . It appears that together with land drainage, many farms and houses were being built or modernised ~ The Lizard becoming popular as a holiday resort.

1861   Bricks were provided for the first Lifeboat House at Polpeor.

1862   Only 13,000 bricks and 250 floor tiles had sold and about 3,000 bricks and 550 tiles were unaccounted for!

1863   We find Pearse Jenkin claiming tax exemption and asking for a rebate. It was clear the business concern was struggling. He wrote ~ 'since commencement of Brick Yard in 1851 the profits have amounted in all to less than £500 and the capital to £1,700. We must appeal against all rates and taxes'.

1863   An Autumn new price list. 'The Company in need of money'. Tenants of Mr Robartes informed they were expected to buy from him.

CHAPTER TWO ~ THE LAND

1864 In February, some 4 tons of large new firebricks sent for from Stourbridge because a kiln needed replacing instantly.

1865 Warning that labour costs at Brick Yard this year must be kept down else total concern will be stopped. Following this, one man dispensed with. George Evans ~ foreman since beginning ~ instructed to burn only three kilns, coal to be rationed! Provision of pipes for the area nearing completion ~ 'sales have been so small that this concern probably to be stopped at the end of year. Demand for bricks not as great as hitherto.'

1866 In January, George Evans told his employment would be terminated at mid-summer. In the meantime was told to make as many bricks as possible, but no pipes. When the yard closed it was suggested that 20,000 bricks should be kept in hand.

1867 Surprisingly in May there is a record of a kiln burn and a new sample of clay sent for trial. George Evans left in August. He had thought of trying to run the yard on his own but Pearse Jenkin glad he gave up the idea. He himself continued to draw a salary until 1868 although that year it was less than a quarter of what it had been.

The closure in 1867 ~ after 16 short years ~ was apparently chiefly occasioned by the demands of the Income Tax Commissioners who could not be convinced that the company was not flourishing despite an Income Tax Appeal held at Helston in 1865 when Pearse Jenkin had spoken out:- 'The concern is not kept open as a speculation but belongs exclusively to Mr. Robartes (Mrs. Agar having meanwhile died). He keeps it going for the convenience of a supply of bricks and pipes for his own farms, all of which is however, charged to him at the going business rate.'

From a map of the period, it seems certain that the present building at the corner of Signal 'Tower' Road, now called 1 and 2 Parc Drae, with its view between Pen Olver and the Lights, was Jeffery's lodging house or Brick House. The entrance to the Brick yard would have been directly opposite this ~ the lane approach being still visible. Brick Yard House (sometimes referred to as Brick House Offices) was in all probability, the now enlarged, 'L' shaped property, known as Brick Cottage which fronts onto Cross Common ~ the Brick Yard being to its rear.   *Irene Wills*

CHAPTER 3

The Sea

~ A WALK ROUND THE COAST ~

To write a book about The Lizard without including the cliffs and the sea would be like writing a book about Scotland without mentioning the mountains and the lochs. To The Lizard the sea has been for many years the lifeblood of the community, through trading, fishing (and wrecking!). Today with its sheer beauty and magnificence it attracts large number of visitors.

The Lizard being one of the last strongholds of the Cornish language has a large number of indigenous names. Some of these are difficult to translate. Others have been corrupted by mispronunciation, misuse or the usage of English cartographers, and leave us with no choice but to make an educated guess at their true meaning.

The parish of Landewednack has a coastline which runs from Kynance Cove in the west via the Most Southerly Point of mainland Britain to Leanwater in the east. What follows is not intended as a definitive guide, but merely as an aid to identification of local landmarks for walkers on the coastal path.

Starting at Kynance Cove (described fully elsewhere in this book) we climb up to pass a small inlet with a holed rock to the north. This bay known as Gertie or Gooly Gazzel (possibly from Goli-Gazel ~ wounded armpit) has claimed at least two lives in falls from the cliffs in recent times. Climbing higher we reach a yellow faced cliff with the formidable figure of the Lion Rock (Ennis vean ~ little island) to seaward. To the south are the broken cliffs of Holestrow (Als-trogh ~ cut or broken cliffs) and beyond, the beach of Pentreath (end or head of beach or sand) with the remains of *The Maud*, her ribs and boilers clearly visible at low tide. At the far end of the beach two fortunate youngsters found some hidden gold bars exposed after a storm. Below this point there is a cave known as Hugo-gwyn (probably white cave) although the pronunciation is close to that of the Cornish for 'wine', leaving room for conjecture.

Passing through the Caerthillian Valley and up to Holseer (Als-hyr ~ high cliff) with its look out post or 'monkey' pole', then on to Old Lizard Head (sometimes said to resemble the profile of the nineteenth century politician Lord Brougham) with its fine view round the coast. Out to sea can be seen many treacherous rocks: collectively known as The Stags (trapped). Immediately below is Kanker-drang (kanker-crab) and the Quadrant. Next seaward are Taylors and the Man of War Rocks (possibly' a corruption of Maen-vere ~ great rock). Furthest out is Mulvin (Moel-ven ~ bare rock). Descending to the next valley we come to Pystyll, once erroneously thought to have derived its name from the 'armed' bodies buried in the meadow. Most likely the name is from Pystyll-ogo (waterfall cave or, just possibly, from Pistole, a Spanish gold coin). The next cove is Polpeor (clear pool) with its disused lifeboat station. The Clidges (possibly Cledger -slope), Labbam Rock and Drang (Lamm ~ leap or jump) and further out Men-hyr (tall stone). Around the grassed area known as the Todden (Tonn ~ grassed area) or The Graves, with Scout's Pool below, we come to Polbream (stinky pool). Above, the lighthouse stands four square to the elements.

Further on is the enigmatic outcrop known as The Bumble, with the Lion's Den on the mainland. This latter is a collapsed cave (1847) which gained its name when a local man wrote the name in white stones. The original two caves can still be seen from the sea. Next we come to Polygick or Bolijack and the Labna-keen or Laven-a-cean (possibly Lamm-kean ~ leap back) or Lavin-keen (back or ridge of a lance). Between here and Housel Bay we have the self-explanatory 'Shark's Teeth'. Housel (possibly Als-howl ~ sunny cliff) is a great favourite with youngsters which accounts for the names of rocks such as Hot Rock and Boys' Rock. Around the Bay to the east is a well-worn hollow known as the wishing well. Then past Carn table and up to Pen Olver (the lookout). The natural amphitheatre here is known as Belidden, above Polleddan, it is said to have been used by Druids for nature worship.

The square building on Bass point is Lloyds Signal Station used in the past to relay messages to and from ships. On the footpath is a red and white brick wall matching a painted area on the buildings, which along with a day mark above Church Cove and a white splash at Hot Point marks the location of the Vrogue Rock, a notorious reef about a mile offshore which has claimed many ships. The path continues past the cove of Green Lane up to Hot Point and then descends steadily to the top of Kilcobben Cove (crooked nook), passing a path down Prilla Ledges, a favourite fishing spot. The new lifeboat, the *David Robinson*, may be viewed here on most mornings.

The path proceeds to Church Cove with its collection of buildings, such as the Cellars formerly used by The Lizard Fishing Company, the Round House used for winching, and an old Lifeboat house used only once during its ten year service. To the eastern side of the cove is Catlyn, another popular fishing spot. In the centre of the bay is a rock known as the Battleship where visitors would alight from passenger ferries out of Helford or Falmouth. To the south are a couple of old mine tunnels, probably used for iron and copper ore.

Following the path up past the Baulk (view point for spotting shoals of fish) another path leads to Penvoose or Parnvoose (probably Porth-fos ~ beach of dyke or wall, or Pen-fos end of dyke or wall). Up the valley is a farm known as An-vos (the dyke or wall). Here the precipitous cliffs have fallen away to leave only signs of a stepped path to the south and a wider track to the north, both now unusable. Back on the main path we have a view of the quarry once used for extracting stone for constructing Predannack Airfield. On the summit the aforementioned daymark can now be seen, erected in 1859 after the sinking of The Czar. The path now descends to the parish boundary at Lean (stitch of land) Water, and the remains of a bamboo plantation.

In this brief description I have attempted to provide an insight into the area and to set in context some of the places mentioned elsewhere in this book. *Nick Pryor*

~ THE LIZARD LIGHTHOUSE ~

Just over half a mile from Lizard Town, as it used to be called, on the exposed southern-most promontory of mainland Britain, stands the well-known Lizard Light. Aloof and solitary, the stark white, octagonal-towered structure guards the hazardous, rock-strewn waters off Lizard Point where lethal, jagged ridges extend for almost a quarter of a mile from the shore.

These waters can quickly become a boiling mass of foam as the sea tears mercilessly at the ragged coast-line. In the world of shipping the stretch of water rounding the Point is renowned for being one of the most difficult to navigate, with more than 200 charted wrecks

CHAPTER THREE ~ THE SEA

on the sea bed to prove it.

Charles Henderson, the eminent Cornish Historian, tells the story of the old sailor who was dying and asked the Vicar to read the passage from the Scriptures 'where they do tell about the Lezar Lights'. Fortunately the Vicar recollecting the verses from Genesis of the 'lesser lights that ruled the night', was able to tell the old man the story of their creation'. Biblical tales apart, the story of The Lizards 'man-made lights' is a venerable one and although the present lighthouse was erected nearly 250 years ago, it was not even then the first building to grace the rugged headland. In 1570 a Sir John Killigrew of Arwenack ~ Arwenack land now being part of the town of Falmouth ~ was granted a Royal Patent by the first Elizabeth permitting him to build a coal-fired light on his own land at Lizard Point.

Sadly massive local opposition prevented this. Publicly it was stated that a light would assist the Spanish Fleet ~ the most likely enemy ~ but there was the less public concern of many that the presence of a light would reduce the number of wrecks and remove a considerable source of their income.

Nevertheless, the project was not forgotten. Half a century later Killigrew's grandson ~ another John ~ with his cousin Lord Dorchester (the British Ambassador to Holland) applied for a similar patent from King James I.

This time, Trinity House joined the locals in opposing the petition, declaring the site to be 'free of outlying dangers, the Channel good, and a lighthouse unnecessary'. Eventually however, the King was persuaded in its favour by Sir Dudley Carleton and the Duke of Buckingham who signed the petition as Lord High Admiral.

Its terms entitled Killigrew jointly with Robert Thynne to erect the lighthouse at their own cost, to maintain it as a charity for 30 years at a rent of 20 nobles a year and accepting only voluntary contributions from passing ships. Erection of another lighthouse nearby was forbidden and a clause added that the light be immediately extinguished the 'moment the enemy is apprehended'.

Sir John's supposedly compassionate gesture met with not a few set-backs. No one locally would work on the tower, the locals relying on 'benefit by ship wreck' ~ an occupation ranging from beach-combing to assault and battery. Killigrew complained to Dorchester that the task was 'far more Troublesome than I expected. The inhabitants near yt think they suffer in this erection. They affirm 'I take awaye God's Grace from them'. They have been so long used to repe by the Callamyte of the Ruin of Shipping as they clayme it Heredytorye and hourly complayne on me'. But he persevered and the lighthouse, built of lime and stone was first lit on Christmas night 1619, the tower having cost £500 to build. The number of shipwrecks fell, but the voluntary contributions never materialised. Sir John soon found himself in financial difficulties, the light was costing 10/- (50p) a night in fuel.

No doubt due to the cost, the light was extinguished for a period of time during 1620 and again in 1621. In 1623 Killigrew received financial help after appealing to the King ~ and this despite Trinity House's disapproval. A compulsory charge of $1/2$d. a ton was levied on all vessels rounding the Point.

There was a terrific uproar at this news, shipowners and merchants alike complaining bitterly and refusing to honour the agreement. It counted little when Sir William Monson, a distinguished and experienced naval officer, spoke out in favour of keeping The Lizard Light. He felt 'It is most fitt seamen should be furnished with as manie other helps as can be devised what a comfort a shipp in distress shall find by this light.'

Despite the King's order in 1623 that 'there should remain a lighthouse forever on that coast' and granting the right to show a light for the duration of the longest life of either Killigrew or Thynne, sometime in late 1624 or early 1625 the light was extinguished, the tower demolished and the patent withdrawn.

There is an interesting twist to the story of Killigrew's lighthouse: shipowners accused him of being a pirate and said the light helped him more than it helped them. Local history also suggests that this particular Killigrew, while posing as the seafarers' friend, was in fact the leader of a band of pirates who operated from the Helford River. His desire for a light on Lizard Point was to ensure that he and not the wreckers should collect the spoils of heavily laden merchant men.

It's certainly difficult to reconcile Killigrews desire to establish a lighthouse to rescue ships with his sentiments about wrecking. In 1627 ill wishers in London actually accused him of piracy and alleged that men under his command had removed cargo from a wreck and threatened death to all who interfered. Sir John informed Dorchester that he had acted thus under his right ~ 'which custom and descent gave me.'

In 1661 a royalist, Captain Edward Penruddock included The Lizard Light in a proposal for several intended lights around the coast, and in 1664, Sir John Coryton petitioned likewise, as did a Henry Brounker. None of these petitions found favour and Trinity House wrote triumphantly that a former lighthouse in that place had been found 'altogether useless.' And so, with passing years, ships continued to pile up on the sea bed around The Lizard.

Trinity House, although founded in 1514 by Henry VIII, took no actual interest in lighthouses until 1565 and even then had no compulsory powers either to levy out or prevent private individuals from building until 1836. Not surprisingly, lighthouses built before then varied considerably in efficiency. By the late 1600's the Elder Brethren had however acquired a respected name and exercised a large say in who should be granted a patent ~ hence their opposition to Killigrew.

Shipping trade increased steadily throughout the 17th and 18th centuries ~ as also did wrecks ~ but Trinity House continued its veto on all proposals.

Then in 1748 a proposal made direct to Trinity House did meet with success. The provisos were for two towers not four and a tenure of 61 years at a rent of £80 a year after which the lighthouse would return in its entirety (including land) to Trinity House. This meant there would be a single light at St. Agnes on the Isles of Scilly, two at The Lizard and three

The Lizard Lighthouse ~ with twin towers ~ and lifeboat house on cliffs above Polpeor prior to 1884 ~

photo P. Mitchell

CHAPTER THREE ~ THE SEA

on the rocks off Guernsey.

A Captain Richard Farish applied for the patent to build the lighthouse on land bought for that purpose by Thomas Fonnereau, an entrepreneur from 'up country'. While gathering signatures to support this petition, Farish fell ill and died but not before he had assigned his rights to Fonnereau.

It has accordingly been recorded that on 24 July 1751 Captains Joseph Cartaret and Edward Smith ~ Elder Brethren proceeded to The Lizard Point at Fonnereau's expense to 'mark out the most proper spot.'

In August of that year the London General Evening Post announced that 'the two brick built towers, having a bearing from each other of W.5N, and E 5.S, and being 72 yards distant, the walls in each case narrowing from 4' at the base to 2'9' at the top, both being 40' in height, were completed. The two lights ~ coal fires behind glass shutters ~ 'will be kindled on the night between 22nd. and 23rd. August and kept consistently burning in the night season'. The two impeccably maintained towers we see today are those same towers which Fonnereau built under the direction of Trinity House nearly 250 years ago.

This being the first lighthouse to be erected on mainland Cornwall, thousands of spectators flocked to see the lights but regrettably the beams were in the main feeble and ineffective. In a largely vain attempt to combat the problem, a cottage had been built between the two towers in which an onlooker lay at night on a kind of couch, from which he could observe both lights through a window at either end. When the firemen in charge of the lights relaxed their efforts at the bellows, allowing the fires to burn dimly, he could recall them to their duties by a blast on a cow-horn.

Once, during the Napoleonic wars, the fires sank so low as to be barely visible. The Captain of a passing Government Packet roused the sleepy watchman by firing a cannon-shot at the dim light.

From 1753 onwards Fonnereau was in dispute with Trinity House over his lease. A long drawn out court dispute resulted which Fonnereau finally lost in 1771. By then he was virtually bankrupt and as no on would take on the remainder of the lease, the Elder Brethren took over the management of the lights themselves. This task has remained their responsibility ever since.

In the early 1800's, the Elder Brethren decided to modernise the lights by substituting oil lamps for the unreliable coal fires. The Royal Cornwall Gazette announcing on January 4th. 1812 ~ 'the necessary lanthorns and apparatus for that purpose are now being erected on the towers, and are expected to be completed on, or about the 16 January next: with the Argand lamps and reflectors producing lights of great brilliance, providing a bright unvarying light all night long and these will be visible to a great distance in every direction'.

Besides modification to the light costing £5,000, the building itself was altered at a cost of £10,000. The two towers were connected by a long range of apartments and offices with a continuous covered passage between them as a protection against the weather ~ in overall structure the lighthouse is largely the same today.

With the increasingly efficient lights, an overlooker was no longer needed and wrecks were considerably reduced. Income for 1852 reached £4,181. 14s. 2d. while expenditure was only £492. 11s. 5d. ~ a handsome profit for the brethren!

Concern was expressed by Trinity House in 1861 that The Lizard Station still had no fog signal, although the Rev. C.A. Johns in 'A Week at The Lizard' 1848 states that an attempt had been made to provide one by means of an experimental steam gun. It is also recorded in that year that the fixed lights in each tower, produced by 19 Argand lamps and parabolic reflectors ~ each 21 inches in diameter and 9 inches deep and made of copper plated with silver ~ were maintained by three light keepers who, were each paid, in descending order of seniority £75, £65 and £45 per annum.

Lake's Parochial History of Cornwall 1865 also records that 'the whole building is whitewashed externally and within each tower is a staircase terminating in a lantern of plate glass set in iron. This iron frame supports these argand lamps which are arranged in two circular rows. The apparatus is so placed that in whatever part of the surrounding ocean a ship might be, at least one of the lights is visible. '

In November 1874 Trinity House decided to introduce Arc lights ~ electricity as such ~ making it only the fourth station to be so equipped. These lights when tested out were enthusiastically reported by the Cornish Telegraph on 5 February 1878; 'The 'electric lights at The Lizard are a decided success. The electricity is produced by a generator, it being composed of a continuous revolving row of magnets against pieces of soft iron, connected with the carbon points, from which the most brilliant of all lights proceeds. The machinery is worked by three steam engines, which take about one hundred and a half of coke to set in motion, after which the machinery will continue to work as long as wanted. It illumines the whole scenery at night for a considerable distance, like the brightness of a summers day. One of these old steam engines used to make electricity is still preserved at the lighthouse today and an arc lamp is to be seen at the Trinity House museum at Penzance. '

The following year, on 13 June ~ a recent collision off The Lizard apparently activating Trinity House ~ a powerful fog siren was decided upon. The West Briton states that a spot has been selected near the edge of the cliff in front of the lighthouse where a steam whistle will be placed as soon as possible. This was duly accomplished ~ the two fog horns being operated by compressed air. On 24 January 1878 The West Briton reported: 'At The Lizard on Sunday, the weather being occasionally very misty, the fog horn was used for the first time in the way of business, at intervals of five minutes. The sound is very weird and melancholy, but landwards, not so loud and disturbing as was anticipated. To those in close proximity however, it must be very annoying, and by night, sleep disturbing. There it rolls, with prolonged reverberating echoes through the surrounding precipices and caves.'

A policy was introduced at that time that the lighthouse keepers should be paid $^1/_2$d. extra per hour whenever the fog horns were in use. This practice continued until the late 1960's, by when the rate had risen to 4d. Officially the fog horns were supposed to operate only when the visibility at sea became less than three miles but locals frequently recounted that the 'dratted noise' could still be heard long after all signs of fog had vanished over the horizon!

The apparatus went into regular service on 29 March 1878 ~ a staff of eight now being required, who with their families made up a small community. The establishment with its varied machinery and fine buildings, was said to enhance the charms of The Lizard for the scientific and sight-seeing tourist. Possibly the practice of showing interested people around the lighthouse began at about this time. Probably it was during this period as well when it was noted that a total of 45 children lived at the lighthouse. The Lady Chapel in Landewednack Church is sometimes known as ' The Trinity ' because it was reserved for the families from the lighthouse who with off duty keepers would regularly attend the Sunday services.

A second electric generator for the lights was added in 1881, this generator having been exhibited at the Paris Exhibition of that year. The lights at that time gave great satisfaction, but not so the fog horns. Wrecks ~ the steamer *'Mosel'* in 1882 and the steamer *'Suffolk'* in 1886 ~ were said to have been both partly attributed to the ineffective horns. The *'Order Book,'* still kept up to date by the keepers, notes that additions and alterations were made on 12 December 1888 to the fog system. From 1895 onwards there were more important modifications, including a Hornsby paraffin oil engine, now also to be seen at Penzance Museum.

In 1903 the light in the western tower was extinguished and removed, with a single revolving optic then installed in the eastern tower. The Wolf and the Longships. (off Land's End) lighthouses had been built by this date, so the precaution taken by Master Mariners of keeping outside the two Lizard towers, in line, to clear Land's End, was no longer necessary. The new light had a lens which was four-sided with 364 prisms and it weighed four tons. This floated in a bath of 800lb. of mercury and was revolved by clockwork driven by a 7cwt weight, giving the lighthouse its own characteristic feature to distinguish it from any other ~ its light now having been increased to 12,000,000 candle power, making The Lizard light the most powerful in the world, emitting a flash every three seconds.

This single brilliant revolving light, first seen at sea on 1 October 1903 immediately gave rise to problems in the village ~ people complaining bitterly they could not sleep because of its intensity. A thick curtain was ordered to be hung permanently on the landward side of the light. Today this is a fixed metal shutter with curtains being drawn during daylight hours on the seaward side to protect the lens from the sun. Three years later the village sent a petition to Trinity House about the brilliance of the light, asking that it should be reduced in power because the brightness had affected the fishing off the coast, a succession of bad pilchard seasons having occurred. Not unexpectedly, Trinity House ignored the request!

The staffing ratio again altered at about this time to one engineer and six lighthouse keepers and such was the interest taken in all this modernisation that on 18 July 1903, the lighthouse was inspected by the then Master of Trinity ~ HRH the Prince of Wales ~ later to become King George the Fifth.

In 1907 J. Harris Stone ('England's Riviera') visited the Station and wrote:- 'The lighthouse possesses four engines, one being the experimental Hornsby oil engine of 1895, and the three others being the very old steam engines. It has two fog sirens, whose character has been altered from two blasts (high and low) every two minutes to two blasts (long and short) every minute ~ the duration of the long blast being seven seconds and the short two seconds ~ this audible ten miles out at sea, dependent on wind and other conditions. In 1908/9 these fog sirens were again altered and the engines updated.

In 1926 the Arc lights were replaced by filament lamps, reducing the candle power to 4,000,000 although The Lizard light was still the strongest in the British Isles with an approximate range of 25 sea miles in clear weather. Also in 1926 the resident engineer departed and the permanent staff was reduced once again to three. There are still only three resident keepers today, Trinity House following a policy of moving them every three years or so to other lighthouses for experience.

Before the war, the domestic facilities for the lighthouse keepers and their families were relatively basic. There were no mod. cons. ~ an earth closet in the back yard and a tin bath before the fire sufficed. All water was by courtesy of rain water butt.

There was electric light only in the downstairs rooms and that only when the generator was running, otherwise it was candles and lamp-light: The four Hornsby Paraffin-driven

CHAPTER THREE ~ THE SEA

engines were still operating the magnets to provide the power for the light, a smaller engine being used to operate the fog horns. The paraffin was brought to the lighthouse by ferry from Penzance in drums, taking a whole day to empty them into a large holding tank. A few years before the coming of the petrol-driven lorry, an old fisherman from Cadgwith, Joe Stephens, described how he had many times carried five gallon drums of oil up to the lighthouse from Bumble Rock where it had been landed by schooner from Penzance ~ no small task!

During the early days of the war, ships were once again ~ as in World War One ~ formed into convoys, these moving at the pace of the slowest, so they took a considerable while to round The Lizard Point. On 28 November 1940, a sea battle took place in which H.M.S. Javelin was set on fire about 15 miles south-east of the lighthouse.

In February 1940 the telephone was installed specifically because the Admiralty needed to give orders when and for how long the light should be shown at night. This light had been reduced to the power of a mere 100 watt bulb which gave a pin prick of light in comparison to the beam which is now seen. Nevertheless this pin prick was sufficient for navigation purposes and even when no light was exhibited, a 24 hour watch was maintained. From November 1940 the lighthouse was camouflaged and I have been told that it was only when the dark brown and green colour had been over-painted in the normal brilliant white that the villagers felt 'the war had truly ended'!

On 11 May 1950 electric current from the National Grid was brought in by help of a step-down transformer. A radio calibrator (for day-time use only) was installed that same year, its call sign being LD LD with a 5 second signal. In July 1954 this calibrator was replaced by a radio beacon ~ call sign LZ making one transmission every six minutes.

The 80's brought further alterations. In 1988 satellite position finders were sited at the station and The Lizard lighthouse commenced monitoring other lighthouses in the area ~ Longships, Wolf Rock, Round Island in the Scillies and the Seven Stones Lighthouse vessel towards the West. Away to the East, the St. Anthony's lighthouse at the entrance to Falmouth Harbour also became automated. All the information now passes through The Lizard station and back to Harwich ~ the nerve centre for all Trinity House lighthouses and lightships. In July 1995 there was a centralisation of all the S.W. Rocks ~ as the automated lighthouses are spoken of within Trinity House ~ the signals now going directly to and from Harwich.

The present Lizard Light gives one flash of 0.1 of a second every 3 seconds, visible from 250 through W to 120 and this will continue to be manned for a further year by the three resident keepers. From 1997 however, both the light and the fog siren will become automatic and although a light will continue to flash and the fog horn to sound it will undoubtedly symbolize the end of an era. An era which will have spanned nearly 250 years, during which time a long line of men have manned The Lizard Lighthouse. Today, 43p. per ton is paid to Trinity House General Lighthouse Fund each time a ship puts into a British port ~ a far cry from when King James I authorized that $1/2$d. a ton per vessel be paid to Sir John Killigrew.

So although for at least half of its long history, the locals apparently fought the existence of this ~ surely one of the most important of all lighthouses ~ it is perhaps a fitting paradox that the last Chief Lighthouse Keeper ~ Michael Matthews ~ should be a locally born Cornishman ~ a true native of 'Lizard Town.'

Derry Dobson with Acknowledgments to Lionel Step.

~ A NOTABLE VISITOR TO THE LIGHTHOUSE ~

Marjorie Povey (nee Wood) recounts from among her memories of a lighthouse childhood of how a few months before war was declared, Von Ribbentrop came and looked over the station, though he did not disclose his identity until her father, Percy, had shown him over it all. 'I remember my father saying he was a very polite and well educated man who showed great interest in everything, and asked many questions. Could he have been spying out the land? Incidentally he gave my Father 10/-, a considerable tip in those days!'

~ THE LIZARD COASTGUARD ~

In 1805 two Naval Lieutenants came to The Lizard to watch out for Napoleon! It could be said that this was the beginning of the Coastguard service in this part of the world. The two men lived in Signal House ~ a small cottage now absorbed into Parc Brawse Hotel. There are two memorials to their memory in the local Parish Church.

In the latter part of the last century the Coastguard Station at Cadgwith, which had commenced its duties in 1875, extended its coverage to The Lizard, building The Lizard West Look Out close to Lizard Head. Coast Guards were gradually rehoused from Cadgwith to The Lizard when houses became available. On the 31 May 1881 Alfred, Duke of Edinburgh ~ second son of Queen Victoria ~ came to the village to inspect and commission two cottages in Penmenner Road. He was accompanied by his Private Secretary and the Inspecting Commander from Falmouth. The following accounts are extracted from records which survive from the 1920's.

It's interesting to read through some of the names ~ familiar to us ~ from the volunteers who manned the Life Saving Apparatus and carried out the rescues under the Coast Guards' instructions. Over the years most able-bodied men of the village considered it an honour to belong to this organisation, the following names being just a few picked at random from the long list ~ Cecil Jose, James Olivey, Percy Emmott, Morley King, Herbert Pascoe, Samual Pascoe, Douglas Tiddy, Sidney Watkins, Stanley Hendy ~ and so the list goes on down to the 60's and further. In 1925 the Look Out Hut at Lizard West was replaced and three new Coastguards' houses built at the top of Penmenner Road.

27 March 1935 ~
French Trawler *Le Vieux Tigre*. Stranded Beast Point, Lizard. 19.51 hrs. received message from Lloyd's Signal Station. Steamer ashore Beast Point Lizard Lifeboat informed 1952 hrs. Called out L.S.A. and proceeded to Beast Point. Found vessel on rocks close in under the cliff. Came into action, fired rocket across vessel but they did not use it. Lizard Lifeboat came alongside and took off the crew of 18 men. No lives were lost. L.S.A. returned and ready for service 0300 hrs. All authorities informed. Awarded £6 for horses, 18 Volunteers @ 17/6d. 2 Coast Guards @ 6/-. Station Officer Cadgwith 12/-.

Several aircraft lost off The Lizard during the war years were recorded by the Coastguards.

21 August 1942 ~
Spitfire Aircraft. $^1/_4$ mile E. of Church Cove. Aircraft crashed into sea ~ no survivors. Observer's body landed at Cadgwith ~ Pilot's body picked up by a vessel and landed at Falmouth.

25 June 1948 ~
U.S.S. Chrysanthystar in collision with fishing boat 'Energetic' PZ.114 in position 10 miles SSE Lizard during thick fog. Two survivors picked up from a crew of seven men, one of whom died later on board *U.S.S. Chrysanthystar*. Cadgwith and Penlee Lifeboats launched. *U.S.S. Chrysanthystar* continued westward, and intercepted by St. Mary's lifeboat in position 49.40 N 6 W; remaining survivor and corpse to land. Weather Fog visibility $^1/_4$ mile. Sea state I Tide $2^1/_2$ hrs. ebb. (U.S.S. United States Steamship.) From the I June 1951 the Coastguard staff took over the role of Lloyds Signal Station, communicating with all the passing trade, by flags or Aldis. Radio communication was taken care of by the Post Office at Land's End.

10 January 1952 ~
Two green star maroons fired at request of Hon. Secretary. Lizard lifeboat launched to stand by *Flying Enterprise* whose tow from 'Turmoil' had parted. Vessel drifting eastwards in rough weather. Other vessels known to be standing by. Only the Captain on board, later mate of *Turmoil* was put on board to assist him. Both men subsequently taken off, and vessel foundered by capsizing in deep water. No lives lost. Weather W. 6 to 7. O.R.Q. (Overcast, rain, squalls) Vis. 5. Sea 4 to 5. Tide 4 hrs. flood. Bass Point Look Out built 1954 and two further houses built at the top of Penmenner.

29 December 1962 ~
The *M/V Ardgarry* ~ a coaster of 600 tons capsized off The Lizard. Lifeboat launched at 2052 hrs. No survivors found. Weather E.N.E. Force 9. Sea 7 Vis. $1^1/_2$ overcast ~ rain. Lifeboat proceeded to Falmouth as it could not be rehoused due to extreme bad weather conditions.

26 August 1966 ~
1728 hrs. Boy over cliff at Kynance Cove. Cliff team proceeded at 1733. On arrival found boy had fallen 40ft. from cliff to beach. Rescue team on Dr's orders carried boy on stretcher up 250 ft. of sloping cliff. Believed suffering from back injuries. Taken to Truro Hospital by waiting ambulance. The boy was on holiday from the Cheshire area.

In later years the Coastguards' watchkeeping duties were taken over by the volunteers known as the Auxiliaries. Coastguard Officers were gradually phased out and re-deployed at M.R.C.C. (Marine Rescue Co-ordination Centres, the nearest centre to The Lizard being Falmouth.) The look out duties were phased out some four years ago although the CRE (Cliff Rescue equipment) is still in existence for continuing cliff and maritime rescues. The National Trust acquired the former Lizard West Look Out in the late 1980's and cleared the entire site, unfortunately leaving no permanent reminder of over 100 years of watch-keeping.

Neville Green.

CHAPTER THREE ~ THE SEA

~ A FRIENDLY COASTGUARD ~

Through the grapevine of a close-knit community Jock Freestone learned of my interest in the sea and invited me to join him during his watches at the Coastguard lookout at Bass Point.

The whole coastline of Britain was covered by look-outs from which the Coastguard officers kept a visual watch for persons or vessels in distress. The officers at The Lizard though had the added responsibility of reporting passing ships to Lloyd's of London, and to the Western Morning News for its much-read column 'Ships Passing The Lizard', as well as supplying local weather observations to the Meteorological Office at Bracknell.

My presence made a pleasant change to the monotony of a familiar occupation and Jock was happy to provide endless anecdotes of his life in the Royal Navy and as a Coastguard officer. 'Well', he would say: 'what do you make of her?' as some vessel would appear around Blackhead or from behind the lighthouse. Still too far off to read her name we would wager her identity based on the information so far available. There was hull form, superstructure and mast dispositions to be considered. Then when hull and funnel colours became visible we would debate ownership. Finally the magnificent telescope mounted on the Aldis lamp was brought to bear on her bows for the tell-tale letters which would confirm or deny our considered opinions.

The Aldis which acted as a mount for the telescope came into its own at night. Perhaps some eighteen inches in diameter, it had louvres operated by a brass side-mounted handle. From it Jack would send Morse with an impressive crispness and speed. Ships would be challenged with a series of A's. Most responded with their names and destination but there were some who were unwilling or unable.

I was allowed to study the station's logbook of passing vessels; Lloyd's List and Lloyd's Register. The Register in two volumes and listing all the vessels of consequence in the world, was a fascinating record of ship's measurement, builders, owners etc. The List published daily, gave only brief details of measurement, but was an indispensable guide of ship movements. Occasionally I was given an old copy, less the end papers. It was, needless to say, a highly valued gift. *William Hocking*

~ BASS POINT COASTWATCH ~

Coastwatch was started in November 1994 by a group called the Sea Safety Group UK, who set up the National Coastwatch Institution because of the worries felt by seafarers all over the country about the Lookout stations being closed down. Bass Point Station was the first one to be reopened and became operational on 18th December 1994, just a month after the NCI sought help from the community. There was much to do to get the Station workable again, as everything had been ripped out at the time of its closure some two and a half years previously, including the electrics, and the place had also been vandalised. A month of hard work and we opened, although the Station was not officially opened until February 1995 when the ceremony was performed by the actress Jenny Agutter.

We have 23 volunteers to date who actively keep watches at Bass Point, but we are always seeking more members to join us, so that we can increase our hours of cover. Our members are unpaid though we try to provide travel expenses for those who come from further afield. Coastwatch Stations are funded purely by public contributions, so each Station has to raise its own funds to meet its costs, which as you can imagine in such a small area can be very difficult.

Lynn Briggs

~ COAST WATCHING ~

(of a different kind)

The sea had, as now, an irresistible fascination and magnetism. I would sit for hours on a grassy ledge beneath the Landmark overlooking Parnvoose and Kennack Bay. On long June evenings it was a joy to watch awesome basking sharks, their gill rakers spread wide, with effortless, powerful sideways swipes of their tails sifting the ocean for krill. Lone fishermen from Church Cove, Cadgwith and Coverack stood at the stern of their small craft jigging for mackerel that, in silvered shoals, rippled the mirrored sea. And Breton langoustiers from Morlaix, Concarneau, Douarnenez and Audierne at anchor for the night, conversed noisily, their voices carrying clear to the shore.

Winter storms were no less fascinating. That same ledge would offer protection from nature's sting. To stand at the cliff's edge a few inches away would take the breath away and salt sting the eyes, where small ships and seabirds sought shelter. *William Hocking*

~ SOME SHIPWRECKS AT THE LIZARD ~

Wrecks and wrecking have always been of great interest to The Lizard people. They even opposed the building of a Lighthouse because they thought it would interfere with their livelihood but it is unlikely though that they ever lured ships ashore with lanterns tied on donkeys' necks walking around the cliffs. Such stories are told but so are lots of others about the Cornish.

There are records of about 100 wrecks from 1800 onwards. Of these about 40 were refloated and so got away.

One of the oldest remains of a vessel still being worked on by divers is known as The Rill Cove Wreck, she is thought to be a 17th Century merchantman, but not yet identified. Many coins have been salved from the reigns of Phillip II and III and represent the first coins minted in the Spanish American Colonies. She was probably a Dutch ship.

On 10 November 1721, the Galley *Royal Anne*, which carried oars as well as sails, was wrecked in bad weather near Pystyll Cove and all but three were drowned. She was taking Lord Belhaven to be Governor of the Barbados and several other persons of distinction. It is thought that about 200 bodies are buried in square communal graves in the meadow ~ Lord Belhaven's body may have been taken home for burial . The three who were saved were said to be local men and a ballad written about the tragedy gives their names as Thomas Lawrence, a boy, George Hain and William Godfrey, and information about The Lizard people at the time. There is now a preservation order on the site.

Not much is known about most wrecks until the mid 1800's when photographs became available and books were written, but a lot of research is being done at present. The first iron

CHAPTER THREE ~ THE SEA

steamer on 22 July 1856, an emigrant ship, the *Zebra*, was a total wreck, but the passengers were probably picked up by Falmouth Tugs.

On 21 January 1859, the steamer *Czar* of Hull 740 tons was wrecked on the Vrogue Rock off Bass Point, and she caused changes which were farreaching. She was being used as a Government transport ship taking ammunition and supplies of uniforms etc to Malta. Some of the crew were saved by the Coastguard Boatmen from Cadgwith and Church Cove and by the local men in their own boats, but the Captain and his wife and child and some of the crew were drowned. The Chief Coastguard John Ridge was afterwards awarded a silver medal by the Board of Trade. Six other men had bronze ones. One came to The Lizard to Samuel Stevens an ancestor of ex-Cox Peter Mitchell, B.E.M. The others received two pounds each. As a result of the loss of life in the wreck of the *Czar*, the Hon . Mrs Agar of Lanhydrock offered to buy a Lifeboat to be stationed on the peninsula. So the first Lizard Lifeboat, (named *Anna Maria* after Mrs Agar) came here in 1859.

On 14 September 1872 there were two Barques, both from Genoa, wrecked on the same rocks the same night. The *Marianna* and the *Nuova Raffalino* left the Far East with cargoes of rice. They met again off the Scillies, then lost each other in fog, only to find themselves on the same rocks when the fog cleared. The crews took to their own boats and made their way to safety. Some of the rice was saved but it soon swelled and the ships were lost.

On 6 September 1879 an early steam ship with sails, the *Brest* of Glasgow, 949 tons went ashore in a fog in Polbarrow. An emigrant ship, she had 130 passengers on their way to Liverpool to join another ship. It was thought at first that some were drowned but they were later found safe. Cadgwith Lifeboat saved some, and these were taken to Falmouth in farm carts with straw to keep them warm. The others were taken by tugs to Falmouth and they all went by train to Liverpool and so to New York.

On 9 June 1882 the Steam Ship *Mosel* of Bremen, 3200 tons, which also carried sails, was wrecked underneath Lloyds Signal Station in fog. An emigrant ship, in later years. she was described.as a 'lovely' wreck ! It was possible to walk aboard from the rocks at the foot of the cliffs. Tugs from Falmouth were soon on the scene and all were safely taken to Falmouth where they went by train to Liverpool and joined another ship to continue their journey to New York.

The *Mosel* had a general cargo of bolts of velvets, brocades and other attractive materials. It was said that these were up every open chimney and behind every gorse bush in the parish, but according to the West Briton of 2 October 1882 it was collected and removed to The Lizard

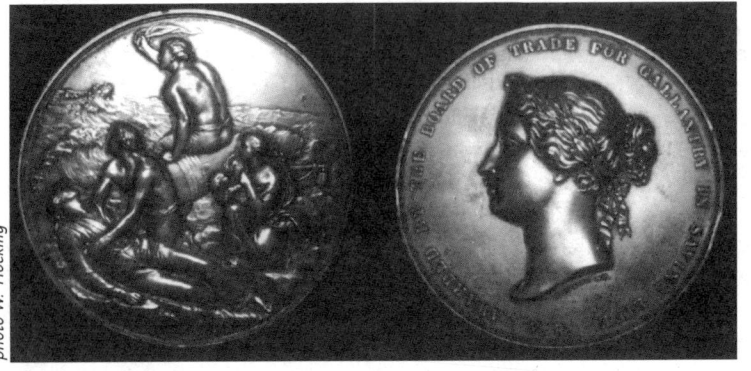

Bronze medal (obverse and reverse) awarded by the Board of Trade to the crews going to the assistance of the *Czar* in January 1859 ~

photo W. Hocking

80 THE LIZARD IN LANDEWEDNACK ~

Green to be taken away! Liberal salvage would be given for materials returned!! Apparently people had been dredging up the materials but it is possible that some were overlooked. One black velvet coat was still being worn in the village in 1930! The ship slipped off into deep water and has been dived on in recent years. Some material has been brought up ~ a very fine woollen, probably 'Nuns' Veiling', which was widely used at the time. Her cargo also included amber pipe stems, pen knives and numerous other attractive collectable items, and there are many photographs of her in existence.

In 1959 a grandson of one of the emigrants came to The Lizard to see where she had been wrecked and to see a photograph of the ship. He took a piece of stone home with him with the hope that it was from the site of the wreck!

On 29 September 1886 another steamer with sails, the *Suffolk* of London, 2924 tons, again in fog was wrecked under Lizard Head ~ her crew were saved by the Lifeboats from Polpeor and Cadgewith, 24 to Polpeor, 21 in the Cadgwith boat. She carried a cargo of sacks of flour and walnut timber and one hundred and sixty three bullocks as deck cargo and four cattlemen to look after them. Some were saved and kept in quarantine in Caerthillian Valley but most of them died. The ones in quarantine were later sold for £9 . 10s ~ £10 each. The ship became a total wreck and her keel can be seen at low tide in calm weather. It was the custom to sell the wrecks and this one was sold to a Falmouth man for £11.

1888 was the year of the ships' Figureheads. Two schooners and one Barque came ashore, and the Figureheads were saved.

On 10 March 1888 the Barque *Lady Dufferin*, 894 tons, of Plymouth struck Mulvin in a gale and it was recorded that the wreckage was on Polpeor beach before the Lifeboat bringing the crew of seventeen got there. Cox. Edwin Matthews received a silver medal for the rescue. The ship which had been built in Prince Edward Island in 1874 was taking rails and sleepers to Argentina for the railway being built there. The Figurehead and some sleepers still remain in The Lizard; but there are no photographs. When wrecks went to pieces at once it was difficult to take photographs.

On 30 July 1888, the Schooner *Robert* of Caernarvon, 76 tons, went ashore very near to Bumble. She was carrying slates from Caernarvon. The crew of four took to their own boat and were saved. The slates were used in the village! The figurehead of a man remained in the village for years but was later sold.

On 29 September 1888, the Schooner *Arab* of Dublin, 84 tons, carrying 180 tons of coal from Swansea to Poole was wrecked at Polbarrow. The seas soon washed over her and the crew of five left her in the ships boat and landed at Caerleon Cove. The figurehead of an Arab woman is still in the village. Between 1900 and 1913 there were several Barques and Sailing Ships lost for various reasons.

On 26 May 1900 the German ship *Wandsbeck* of Hamburg, 1782 tons, was a total wreck off Polpeor in calm weather having got caught in the tides. Laden with wheat she soon broke up and was bought by a Falmouth man for £55. The crew took to their own boats.

On 11 November 1900, a Norwegian Barque, the *Glimt*, 424 tons of Stavanger went on the rocks also at Polpeor but this time in very bad weather. She broke up so quickly that it was a difficult rescue. The Lizard and Cadgwith Lifboats saved all the crew but the cabin boy refused to go to sea again ~ he remained in Cadgwith for some years and was known as Robert Glimt.

Another Norwegian sailing ship, the *Hansy* of Fredrikstad, 1497 tons had missed stays in

Housel Bay on 3 May 1911 and this caused her to be blown on to Carn Table, a rock between Housel Beach and Pen Olver. The Captain's wife and child and two crew were rescued by the Rocket apparatus and the others by The Lifeboat. She was laden with timber flooring and other boards on her way to Sydney, Australia to build houses. The timber all washed into Housel and a lot was saved and used in the village.

In 1912 on 11 February the steam Trawler *Maud* of Fleetwood, 79 tons, was on tow by the tug *Challenger* when the tow broke and with no-one on board the *Maud* drifted on to Pentreath Beach ~ where her boiler and keel can still be seen at low tide. She had previously been ashore on the Isle of Man and was being taken to Hull but the gale broke her tow. There was a court of inquiry at Liverpool and several Lizard men had to attend but the findings are lost in the mist of time!

On 15 May 1913, the beautiful Barque *Queen Margaret* of Glasgow, 2144 tons, had the misfortune to go ashore, again at Polpeor, while waiting for orders from Lloyds Signal Station. She was carrying a cargo of wheat which soon swelled and caused her to break up. The captain and his wife and child were saved by the Lifeboat and the crew came ashore in the ship's boats.

Then eight days later on 23 May 1913, the sailing ship *Cromdale*, 1903 tons of Aberdeen came in with all her sails set in thick fog at Bass Point. Seven of her crew were saved by The Lizard Lifeboat and twenty by the Cadgwith boat. She was carrying nitrate and soon became another total loss.

The most serious disaster between 1900 and 1913 was the wreck of White Star Liner *S.S Suevic* of Liverpool of 12000 tons with a crew of one hundred and forty one and three hundred and eighty two passengers on 17 March 1907 on Maenhere ledges off Polpeor in thick fog. Cadgwith Lifeboat was credited with saving two hundred and twenty seven lives and The Lizard with one hundred and sixty seven and this record for saving lives by the RNLI still stands. Help in the rescue was also given by the Porthleven and Coverack lifeboats. The R.N.L.I. awarded silver medals to Cox. W.E. Mitchell and 2nd Cox. Edwin Mitchell of The Lizard boat and Cox. Rutter and the Reverend H. Vyvyan, Hon. Secretary, of the Cadgwith one. Two of the ships' crews also were awarded Silver Medals for carrying the children (of whom there were many) to the boats.

The *Suevic* also carried cargo of wool and mutton. The wool was salvaged from various beaches and together with other pieces of cargo was collected on the Green and each man sold what he had saved, and there was a tremendous crowd on the Green to witness the sale. There are photographs showing Polpeor dressed with flags. The lifeboat was launched to take Lord and Lady Clifton around the wreck. The Land for the Boat house had been given by the family, so presumably this was showing appreciation for the gift and for the first Lifeboat The Anna Maria.

After much consultation it was decided to cut the ship's bow off and leave it on the rocks ~ the rest of the ship was towed to Southampton. A new bow built in Belfast was towed to Southampton and the two pieces were joined together. The *Suevic* sailed for many more years ending up as a Finnish Whaler. She was scuttled in 1942 in the North Sea to prevent her being captured by the Germans.

There were several ships lost by enemy action in 1917 and early 1918 and afterwards there seemed to be a lull. Then on 9 February 1923 the *Adolph Vinnen of Bremen*, 1529 tons was lost in a severe gale in Green Lane Cove. She was a five mast auxiliary schooner on her maiden voyage with insufficient ballast and was blown ashore ~ her German crew were rescued by the Rocket apparatus in the morning. The Lifeboat, the new motorboat F.H. Pilley could not get near enough in the rough sea to rescue them ~ neither could she return to Polpeor for the same reason, but had to go to Falmouth for shelter. The *Adolph Vinnen* became a total wreck. Many spoons and forks and other things remained in use in the village for a long time, all with the ship's name and flag on them. In June of the same year the steamer *Nivelle*, 993 Tons of London came into Pentreath in thick fog. Her crew of twenty were saved by the *Pilley*. She was laden with coal and it was dumped on the beach. At low tide it could be carried away and dragged up the cliff. One farmer had 30 tons but it didn't burn very well in the Cornish Range; a lot of people had a few baskets full! The *Nivelle* was refloated and so saved to sail again.

The *Pilley* had previously saved the crew of 23 of the *St Patrice of Swansea* on 21 May 1922, a tanker, of 1968 tons, again in fog, stranded on Mulvin Ledges. She was towed away but sank in the North Sea on her way to be repaired in Germany.

On 31 August 1924 the *S.S. Bardic* of Liverpool, another White Star Liner, was wrecked on Maenheere near where the *Suevic* had gone ashore in 1907 in thick fog. The *Bardic* had a cargo of frozen rabbits. Her crew of ninety three were brought ashore in the Lifeboat. When it seemed safe some men went back on board to keep the refrigerators working but on 8 September 1924, the wind got up and 44 crew came ashore in the lifeboat. The refrigerators stopped working and when the ship was pumped out to refloat her the smell was awful! She was towed to Falmouth for temporary repairs and the rabbits were taken out and dropped down a mineshaft somewhere near St.Day!

This was the last time that Cadgwith men in the crew were met at Trethvas by the *Waggonette* and *Swallow* ~ after that a car was used.

Another lull and then in 1935 there were three ships wrecked, all in fog.

On 27 March 1935, *Le Vieux Tigre,* a steam trawler of Bologna came in on the same spot as the *Mosel* in 1882. Her crew of eighteen were the first to be rescued by the new Lifeboat the *Duke of York* ~ the trawler slipped off into deep water and became a total wreck.

On 20 June 1935 the *D L Harper* of Danzig after about eighty hours of fog struck the Crane Ledges. Her crew of 43 and a baby were brought into Polpeor by the Lifeboat. She proved very difficult to move from the rocks but after several tugs including a large Dutch one and another tanker were employed together she was safely taken to Falmouth for repairs. She was beautifully equipped in the crews' quarters and altogether very modern for the times.

On 26 September of the same year the *Clan Malcolm* of Glasgow, laden with maize, was wrecked near Hot Point. Her crew took the boats and went to Cadgwith. Her fittings were taken to Cadgwith and sold by auction on the beach. Finally as she was considered a danger to shipping she was blown up and sunk.

These are some of the wrecks in living memory and some kept alive by stories from the previous generation. Some ships stayed on the rocks for days or weeks and brought many people to the village to see them. In some cases the farmers charged for cars to use farm lanes to reach the cliffs for a better view!

One ship, the *S.S. Skjoldborg* of Haugesund on January 18, 1920 was only visible for a very short time. Her crew took to their own boat and the man who saw her aground went home to lunch and when he got back to Polpeor she had disappeared into deep water, so there was no chance of going aboard to salvage anything! Lizard people are said to have greatly benefited from one shipwreck according to Mr. Hunt's *Popular Romances of the West of England* first published in 1881, *The Lizard People*:

'There is a tradition that The Lizard people were formerly a very inferior race. In fact it is said that they went on all fours, till the crew of a foreign vessel, wrecked on the coast, settled among them and improved the race so much that they became as remarkable for their stature and physical development as they had been for the reverse. At this time (1881) as a whole, The Lizard folks certainly have among them a very large population of tall people, many of the men and women being over six feet in height!'

Joan Hart

~ UNCLE HOWARD ~

Among those I secretly admired and whose company I enjoyed was Howard Mitchell. Howard was very much a jack of all trades. There were few jobs in the parish that he had not tried his hand at. When I knew him he was a serpentine turner but was always happy to oblige anyone in need of casual help. He welcomed the diversion of attending to the needs of Trinity House or of farmers requiring extra hands on threshing days or at harvest time. He enjoyed the social contact which he lacked behind the lathe.

Given an attentive audience, Howard was a willing raconteur and would regale listeners with tales of old for which he had an excellent memory. I always enjoyed his reminiscences, particularly those relating to the sea, and invited him to view my recently acquired collection of Gibson wreck photographs. His eyes lit up and. after a momentary pause of disbelief that anyone should share his passion for such a subject, burst into an excited monologue:

'You can't remember ~ no! you can't? oh well ~ you've heard tell of 'n ~ William Edward up to Cadgwith. Well he was coxswain of the lifeboat then, see. She (the *S.S. Suevic*) came in 1907, 17 March.

Well, what they done, they went up on the downs and they bagged up quite a lot of clay to take out to put down for the divers for blasting. They blast her in two, see? So, I was a boy and amongst the lifeboat helpers ~ a telephone boy I was ~ and old William Edward said, 'You jump aboard boy, and with this book and pencil count how many bags we've sent up, see?

I went out and they started sending up three bags at a time and I would put down three and up goes three more and I would put down six and so on.

He said, 'How 'e getting on boy?'
'Alright', I said.
'What are'e doing of 'n?', he said.
'Why, counting the bags as you told me to'.
'Ah, that ain't the way to do it', he said. 'Gimmee the pencil. Look! You do it like this one, two, three, four and then a scat across and we add them up in fives'.

It was clear that Howard enjoyed adventure for he later abandoned the building of a mangold rick to witness the destruction of the *Hansy* under Carn Table, Housel Bay in May 1911. He put this desire to be in the middle of the action to good effect for the R.N.L.I. as brakeman and was delighted to shake hands with the Duke of Edinburgh at the opening of the new lifeboat station at Kilcobben in 1962.

William Hocking

CHAPTER THREE ~ THE SEA

~ THE LIFEBOAT ~

Since 1859 the lifeboat has been part of The Lizard life. Stationed at Polpeor, the most southerly point in England, and after 102 years, moved to Kilcobben to the East of the Point.

It has progressed from a small six-oared boat to the present twin-engined one with wonderful accommodation for the crew and any rescued people. All the small lifeboats were known as pulling and sailing as they carried sails as well as oars.

The first boat came to Polpeor in 1859 ~ the gift of the Hon. Mrs. Agar of Lanhydrock, who had been so affected by the wreck of the *Czar* on 24 January 1859 and the loss of life from it, that with the help of her land agent the site at Polpeor was chosen for a lifeboat. The first of three *Anna Marias* named after Mrs. Agar was kept in a house on top of the cliff (Todden) on a carriage, on which she was let down to the beach and brought up again. At the acute turn in the road down to the beach there was a large tank of water sunk into the ground (with a large wooden bollard beside it) to cool the rope as the boat was let down and when she was hauled up afterwards. The remains of the bollard are still there.

She was small with only six oars as there were not enough fishermen to man ten. She cost £135 with her carriage and was 30' by 6' by 3'3" and weighed 30 c.w.t. The *Anna Maria* was brought overland by the different railways then existing, and the carriage could be drawn by horses, on one occasion being taken to Mullion across the downs to a wreck, but sadly arriving too late to save the crew.

The services carried out by the lifeboats were recorded on large black boards at Polpeor and it must be stressed that only when lives were saved, or help given to saving ships, were services shown on the boards, so people reading these had no idea how often the crews had put to sea, sometimes in the most terrible of conditions.

Only one service was recorded for the first *Anna Maria* and then while out on a practice she was smashed by the heavy seas and the Cox. Peter Mitchell and second Cox. Richard Harris and crew member Nicholas Stevens were drowned. There was a collection made for the families and the R.N.L.I. contributed £130.

The *Anna Maria*, donated by T.J.Agar Robartes of Lanhydrock, on its carriage at Polpeor ~

photo J. Hart

The second *Anna Maria* appears to have been supplied by the R.N.L.I. She also had six oars but was 6" wider, which may have made her safer. She cost £303 with a carriage. Between 1868 and 1875 she saved 13 people and went out on 5 services. She was withdrawn after the last one as she was damaged during the launching.

~ THE LIZARD IN LANDEWEDNACK **85**

CHAPTER THREE ~ THE SEA

The third *Anna Maria* was the gift of Lord Robartes and cost £325. She was slightly larger and the oarsmen were double-banked and there were ten of them. She performed three services and saved 36 and was transferred to Church Cove where a house had been given as a refuge. The lifeboat house at Church Cove was built in 1877 by three cousins in memory of Thomas Chavasse Esq. F.R.C.S., his wife and two others. It was hoped to use it as a refuge for the *Anna Maria* when she could not get back into Polpeor in bad weather. The *Anna Maria III* was transferred from Polpeor in 1885 and was replaced by the *John and Sarah* in 1887. Only two services were recorded and the station closed in 1899. The house having cost £291 to build was then sold for £40.

In 1884 the road down from the village was built up at a cost of £200, the new Boat House ~ later the winch house ~ was built, and the sea wall was plastered and the date inscribed on it.

Then another new boat, the *Edmund and Fanny* came. She was the gift of Mrs. Holland of London and cost £366, only slightly larger and with 10 oars double banked ~ ie. two men on each thwart. Her coxswain was Edwin Matthews who was awarded the R.N.L.I. Silver Medal for the rescue of the crew of the Barque *Lady Dufferin* on 10 March 1888. She is credited with saving 74 lives.

The next one was the Admiral Sir George Back costing £780. A larger boat 35' long by 8'6' again having 10 oars and paid for by the legacy from Mrs Eliza Back of Midhurst. The first service was in 1907 to the *S.S. Suevic*. Her coxswain was William Edward Mitchell from Cadgwith as were two or three others of the crew. The second coxswain was a Lizard man, Edwin Mitchell, and they both received the R.N.L.I. silver medal for the rescue of passengers from the *Suevic*. This lifeboat remained at Polpeor until 1918 with 234 lives to her credit.

In 1914 the launching slipway for a motor lifeboat had been started with a new boat house and turn table to make it possible to bring her on to the beach bow first. All the pulling and sailing boats had come in stern first so they were then ready for re-launching down the old slip-way again. By 1918 the new house and slip-way were ready and the R.N.L.B. Sir Fitzroy Clayton was lent to the station from Newhaven. She had been built in 1912 for £3,081. Much larger than the rowing boats she weighed 8 tons 15 cwt.

In 1914 Mr. F.H. Pilley had given £5,000 to the Institution to provide the new boat house, slip and motor boat for The Lizard, but owing to the 1914-1918 war there was a delay. By the time the *F.H. Pilley* (named after him) arrived in 1920 and Mr. Pilley was ill, and his daughter performed the naming ceremony on 18 August 1922. The Rector conducted a short service of dedication and a bouquet of flowers was presented to Miss Pilley by Joan Jenner. Quite a crowd came to see this ceremony, the lifeboat was very much part of the community life of the village ~ perhaps even more so than it is today.

The *'Pilley'* as she became known had a crew of eight. Her Coxs. was Richard 'Jarvis' Stephens of Cadgwith and for the first time a full time mechanic W. Stephens also of Cadgwith was employed, a house being provided for him and his family at The Lizard.

This boat and her crew perfomed many gallant services and she stayed here until 1934 when her place was taken by a twin engined boat given by the King George's Fund for Sailors at a cost of £5,636 and weighing 14 tons 10 cwts. She was named *The Duke of York* by the Countess of Shaftesbury. The invitation called it the *Inaugural Ceremony* on 22 June 1934. The boat was lowered half down the slip and chairs were arranged behind it up the slip and into the house for ticket holders.

The two engines gave the crew much more confidence and there was a cabin for the mechanic and his engines and for the Coxs. to have some protection from the sea and weather. The Coxs. of the *Pilley* had had to hang onto the wheel, not only to steer the boat but to save his life in bad weather against which there had been no shelter at all!

A photo taken after a service of 'standingby' the *S.S. Runnelstone* in July 1934 shows five Cadgwith men and three Lizard men in the crew. From the very beginning of the lifeboat service Cadgwith men had always been part of the crew. In 1935 there were three ships ashore. In March the *Le Vieux Tigre*, a French trawler under Lloyds Signal Station became a total wreck and the crew of 18 men were safely brought into Polpeor. On 20 June the tanker *D.L. Harper* struck the Crane Ledges in thick fog. Her crew were brought in by the *Duke of York*. Although the oil had drained out very quickly, it didn't appear to do any damage. On 26 September more fog caused the *S.S. Clan Malcolm* to be wrecked off Hot Point. Her crew went into Cadgwith in their own boats so the lifeboat only 'stood by'. The ship became a total wreck and was finally blown up, as she was a danger to shipping. All her fittings etc. that could be salvaged were sold on Cadgwith beach by auction.

After the record breaking three wrecks in one year, Ernest 'Lambey' Stephens took over as Coxs. from Jarvis in 1938 and the *Duke of York* saved six from the *S.S. Rubaan* in December 1939. During the war years there were a few times when the boat went out. In 1941 there was a ship sunk by enemy action but when the lifeboat reached the scene there was nothing and nobody to be found. There were other occasions when she went out to stand by and on one such occasion she picked up a German airman.

In 1952 George Mitchell, also of Cadgwith became Coxs.in time to try to help the *S.S. Flying Enterprise* which had broken her tow some miles off the Point. It was an atrocious night and Mr. Chapman the Hon. Sec. went with them. His description of the fruitless journey can be read in 'The Lizard Lifeboat Centenary Year 1859 -1959.' The *Duke of York* stood by until the petrol got low and she had to go to Falmouth to refuel. Almost at once the two men still aboard the *Flying Enterprise* jumped off the funnel, which by that time was almost flat on the sea and they were picked up by the tug which had been towing them. Because of heavy sea, it had been impossible to reconnect the tow rope. After this, the calls were mostly from yachts and small fishing craft which needed help for various reasons.

1959 was the Centenary year so the R.N.L.I. held a short service at Polpeor. The lifeboat was dressed with flags and the crew wore the traditional red caps. Sadly, these are no longer worn on such occasions. Crowds of people came to the ceremony and special constables directed the traffic. The road had been made up in 1952 and so cars could get to Polpeor easily.

In 1958 work had started at Kilcobben. A wave counter had been used for two years to prove that that cove was the safest place to build a new house and slip-way. There was a large rock in the middle of the cove where a Seine boat had been kept in the Pilchard fishing days. This was the foundation for the new house and the slipway was built out from it. The building materials were brought by sea and the work went well. A lift was installed and worked from the engine house at the top of the cliff. Steps with hand rails were built from the Boathouse to the top of the cliff where a small car park was made. A new road was built across the fields from the road to Church Cove . Altogether it was a tremendous undertaking but it has proved to have been a wise decision. The only drawback is that it seems a long way to run when the rockets are fired!

The new lifeboat arrived in October 1960 and was named *The Duke of Cornwall* by H.R.H The Duke of Edinburgh, who arrived in a red helicopter on 7 July 1961. Stands were erected for

CHAPTER THREE ~ THE SEA

invited guests and very many watched from the cliffs.

The boat, a 52' Barnett Class was the gift of the Civil Service No. 33. She was much larger than the *Duke of York* and had much more sheltered accommodation for the crew and rescued people.

She was also faster and had a much longer range and was equipped with the latest radar etc. George Mitchell continued as Coxs. until 1967 and took the boat out on 7 January 1963 ~ another dreadful night ~ to look for the *S.S. Ardgarry* in trouble off Polpeor. By the time they had arrived at the position given however, the ship had sunk and no survivors could be found. On 8 January 1963 The Times printed a photo of one of the *Ardgarry's* ship's boats washed ashore at Sennen Cove. That was one of the worst services a lifeboat can do.

In 1967 Bunny Legg became Coxs. The anticipation of shipwrecks had gradually died down. The village and crew got used to the calls from yachts and small fishing craft, sometimes in severe weather. The *Duke of Cornwall* and various boats which came to the station while she was away for a re-fit responded to 88 calls and brought in over 90 people and towed or escorted numberless vessels to safety.

In 1984 it was decided to replace the *Duke of Cornwall* with the ex-Padstow boat, the *James and Catherine McFarlane*. She was rededicated at Kilcobben on 1 August 1984. A short prayer of thanks was given for the 24 years of service given by the *Duke of Cornwall*. The *James and Catherine McFarlane* stayed here until the new Tyne Class *'David Robinson'* arrived in 1988 ~ the naming and dedication of which took place on 13 May 1989. She was named *David Robinson* by Mrs. Jean Baker, the daughter of the Donor ~ the late Mr. David Robinson ~ who had also given the *'Mabel Alice'* named after his wife and stationed at Newlyn.

The *Tyne Class* boats are 'fast slipway boats' and all are well equipped for the safety and comfort of the crew and casualties ~ if the Coxs. of the *Pilley* could see it he would be amazed. The *David Robinson* has proved to be much faster and have a greater range than the previous boat. She has given help to many yachts and fishing vessels in some severe gales and will continue to do so for some time.

Up to January 1995 the crew had assembled 89 times, saved 54 and landed eight, had some false alarms and saved property worth many thousands of pounds. Peter Mitchell had become Coxs/Mechanic in 1976 and was awarded the R.N.L.I. Bronze medel for the rescue of the yacht Bass on September 3 1984 whilst Coxs/Mech. of the *James and Catherine McFarlane*. The medal was presented to him at the A.G.M. in London on 2 May 1985.

In April 1986 Coxs/Mech. P. Mitchell was awarded the B.E.M. for his 34 years service to the Institution. The presentation was made by the Lord Lieut. of the County of Cornwall, Lord Falmouth, at the Polurrian Hotel on 22 April 1986.

In 1988 he was succeeded by Phillip Burgess whose Grandfather had served in the *Duke of York* in 1934. The crew are mostly Lizard men who have all sorts of jobs but when the rockets go (though they all have bleepers now) they all leave these jobs and dash down to the boathouse whatever the weather. The Hon. Sec. or the Deputy Launching Authority gives the word to launch and the Head Launcher 'knocks the pin out' and away she goes. They have radio which keeps them in touch with Falmouth Coastguards who give them the position of the casualty. R.N.A.S. helicopters usually help them and recently the Doctor was transferred by the helicopter to tend an injured man on the ship in a bad gale and the man was then taken to hospital ~ not a very pleasant experience for the Doctor!

There are shore helpers under the Head Launcher, who launches the boat and helps to bring her on to the slip by attaching the hawser to bring her up to the house after a service or practice. She is at once got ready for service again ~ hosed down, examined for damage and refueled ~ whatever the time!

There have been several gold and silver badges awarded to Committee members and Ladies' Life Boat Guild officers for Service to the Institution and very many Thanks on Vellum to the crew and helpers for gallantry and long service.

And so the service to those in peril on the sea continues and will continue while there are young men willing and able to man the lifeboat.   *Joan Hart*

~ ON EXERCISE IN A LIFEBOAT ~

I have to admit that it was not my idea to take a trip on a lifeboat. It was the brain-child of my old school friend, Malcolm Jones. His parents ran a camp and caravan site on which were strategically placed collecting boxes for the RNLI. Evidently the campers proved generous to the point that the Hon. Treasurer of The Lizard-Cadgwith branch offered Malcolm a trip, the date to be arranged. Malcolm's enthusiam for adventure no doubt seeded the idea! His second great idea was that I should accompany him! In support of this I was assured that my deep sea experience would hold us in good stead.

The chosen day, a Wednesday in darkest January, broke with leaden skies and a rising wind. By lunchtime rain splattered noisily on the glass and the windows rattled in their sashes. I ate my pasty heartily, confident that my friend would see reason and abstain from this foolhardy venture. I was wrong! In burst Malcolm propelled by enthusiasm and a fierce gust of wind. I was carried away still devouring the remnants of my meal.

At the lifeboat station we and some cadets from RNAS Culdrose were issued with oilskins and life-jackets and mustered in the cockpit aft. Coxswain George Mitchell, satisfied that his crew were at their appointed stations, cried 'Stand Clear!'. With a deft swing of his hammer, the launcher sent the pin ringing from the mooring chain.

The *Duke of Cornwall* surged forward, gathering the momentum necessary to throw her clear of the slipway and the treacherous cliffs of Kilcobben Cove. The bow dug deep before the stern sprang free of the slipway. She pulled up short, her bow breaking the surface casting a torrrent of water above those clutching the handrails around the exposed cockpit. With a shudder she shook the remaining water from her decks and purposefully forged a course for Blackhead.

The engines purred with authority, propelling the craft with an easy motion across Kennack Bay, as yet hardly ruffled by the gale that was blowing to the westward. The exhilarating plunge now turned into a pleasant trip around the bay.

Before reaching Blackhead Coxswain Mitchell turned his charge for home. I was now happy that my earlier misgivings about the venture were unfounded and, indeed, was quite enjoying the experience! Imagine my horror when coxswain Mitchell chose not to seek the warmth of the boat-house but to proceed around the corner into the full fury of the gale. I felt like a jockey on a runaway horse. There was no getting off.

Abeam of Polpeor the gale force winds sent streamers along the surface of the tormented sea. Spray and spume obscured the land from view. The *Duke of Cornwall* twisted and corkscrewed like a wild animal on a leash. No big ship motion was like this. We seemed to be more under water than above it. All the while we clung to the boat with backs to the wind and sea and yet salt water penetrated every orifice of clothes and body. Muscles and stomachs ached in their fight against the mad motions. The cockpit floor was awash with water and vomit.

I was spared the retching. A stomach full of pasty and a crew who engaged me in conversation took my mind off the worst of the pangs. And yet I had ample time to contemplate the power of the sea and the historic shipwrecks on rocks only yards away. The Man o' War and its brothers loomed dark and sinister above the seething sea. Gigantic fingers of white water clawed at Old Lizard Head as though to envelope it in its evilness. To seaward I glimpsed a great wall of water tumbling into a hissing mass.

While fellow passengers around me thought only of hell, I dismissed fear of my situation knowing full well that I was in the best of hands. The boat was of a trusted design, built by craftsmen, and capable of self-righting and unsinkable. The crew were bold but experienced and led by a coxswain who instilled unflinching trust in all who served under him. For a service steeped in history and tradition there can be no other way.

This trip, which started out as a joyride, matured in the space of two short hours into a voyage of understanding and respect for those who volunteer, in fair weather or foul, to venture forth to help their fellow men. *William Hocking*

~ HENRY TRENGROUSE ~

On 29 September 1807 the frigate *Anson* was driven ashore in a terrific gale on the Loe Bar, Helston. Upwards of 60 men were drowned whilst onlookers watched, powerless to help.

Henry Trengrouse, one of those onlookers, never forgot this and, it is said while watching a firework display, the idea came to him of attaching a cord to a rocket which would be fired from the land to a ship. By this means the crew could be drawn to safety.

At The Lizard the first Rocket House was built in 1869. In 1967 it was moved to a new building beside No.1 Coastguard Cottages at the top of Penmenner Road. Three years ago the equipment was moved to Mullion where it is kept at the ready on a mobile Land Rover.

~ THE LIFE SAVING APPARATUS ~

I can remember the Rocket Apparatus as far back as 1921. It was kept in the Rocket House opposite the Chapel ~ Ken Bright now has this premises for his 'Auto Repair Business'.

There were three sections ~ rocket, whip and anchor. The crew for many years was Hector Pitman No.1, Bert Pascoe No.2, Harry Bray No.3 (rocket), S.Watkins (anchor), P. Emmott, Alf Menear, Fred Harris, Elvyn Bray, H. Bray (Little Gent), and Herbert Bray.

In the main, Tregominion Farm supplied the two horses. For a few years Mr Richards from Hellarcher farm might have had the largest and heaviest horses and I remember Mr Barrett also supplied a lorry for a year or two, then it went back to Mr Hendy at Tregominion ~ and so it went over the years. During the War Hellarcher was licenced to have a tractor with rubber tyres for pulling the apparatus up and down the lane. Everyone else had to make do with 'spade luggs' on their wheels.

The first 'call out' I can remember was to the *Adolf Vinnen*. My Dad took me down to Green Lane Cove on his shoulders. Somewhere in the village there is a photograph of Herbert Pascoe taking a man out of the Breeches Buoy from this wreck. It was a cold easterly wind and whilst waiting for orders from Lloyd's Signal Station she 'mistayed' and came ashore before they could start her engines. Five Germans stayed in the rigging most of the night ~ it being 1923 and only a few years after the war, they were frightened of the English and what they might do to them!

The rocket was called out by the Coastguards who fired one maroon; the lifeboat was called out by two maroons if it were needed. When all three maroons were fired there was great excitement in the village, with both rescue services running to Station, along with every able bodied person in the village ~ or so it always seemed ~ hurrying to see the wreck.

It was very difficult at times firing a line out to the wreck. If it was windy, the line would easily blow away from the ship. Hector Pitman was a good shot and never missed. Several lines were fired to ships at various times but not always used, as ships sometimes got away with help from tugs.

One ship I remember ~ the *S.S. Nivelle* came into Pentreath. A rocket was fired which landed on her whistle! This blew nearly all night until the steam ran out. That ship stayed at Pentreath for several weeks, unloading coal on the shore side of the ship. All the village had plenty of coal for the next year or two! We were five brothers in our family and father had us all carrying coal in our spare time. The ship was eventually refloated and towed away by *The Lady of the Isles* on the 25th June 1923.

My brother Reg and I joined the L.S.A. in 1946 but previous to the War we had for some years both been in the lifeboat (*The Duke of York*). At one time there had been three sets of brothers in the crew ~ Lamey and Tog Stephens, George and Robert Mitchell, and Reg and myself. Then there were also Harry Curnow and Eddie Matthews in the crew.

The L.S.A. acquired its own Land Rover in 1951 which was kept at the Coastguard Station. We were also a cliff rescue squad. In my career of 34 years I had over 200 call outs.

The last crew members I remember working with were R. Johns, B. Mitchell, R. Stephens, D. Pitman, D. Hocking, N. Green, T. Hendy and C. Hendy.

Cliff rescues are much easier these days thanks to the Navy Choppers but in its time Henry Trengrouse's invention of the Rocket Apparatus was a greatly needed service offered to all men in danger of losing their lives.   *Arthur Johns.*

~ PASSING THE LIZARD ~

Both before and after Killigrew thought of building a Lighthouse in 1619, The Lizard Point has been associated with shipping, the first and last landfall for the sailing ships which were away for weeks or months at a time. After 1872 when returning vessels were in sight of Lloyd's Signal Station the signal flags were hoisted to identify the ships to the station and to ask for orders from the owners for the disposal of the cargoes. The signalman at Lloyd's would telegraph to the owners for instructions which were then sent by flags to the ships. As sailing ships were replaced by steamers, Lloyd's continued to signal by flags and to report the arrival of ships to the owners.

CHAPTER THREE ~ THE SEA

At night an Aldis lamp was used with morse code from a look-out below the station to avoid the flashing of the Lighthouse light. These methods were used until most ships had radio and the station closed in 1951.

Almost my earliest memory is of a ship being hit by a German torpedo in 1917. She was probably the *Bellucia*. She drifted up channel and sank east of Church Cove and is now a good site for fishing. She was laden with sacks of flour and wheat; some of these were landed but only a small amount of flour was dry in the middle of the bags. It was at this time too that small airships were stationed at Bonython for submarine spotting. They flew over the gardens to the sea and the men could be seen in the basket hanging from the balloon.

After the first World War when things got back to normal the large liners came back on the North Atlantic service to New York and they were joined by some taken from the Germans in reparation.

The white star liner *Majestic* with three yellow funnels had been the German *Bismarck*. During the 20's and 30's she was a most popular ship with the regular passengers. The Cunard liner *Mauretania*, with four red funnels had been built in 1907 and held the Coveted Blue Riband for the fastest crossings of the Atlantic until 1929 when she lost it to the *Bremen* of the Norddeutscher Lloyd line. The *Mauretania* was withdrawn from service in 1935 and was broken up at Rosyth.

The second *Mauretania* with two funnels was on the North Atlantic run from 1939 to 1965. She did great service as a troopship during the Second World War and after a re-fit she returned to her old route for a short time and then went cruising in the Caribbean.

In the early 20's the White Star line *Olympic* with four yellow funnels came closer to the shore than most and we thought that as one of the stewards was a Lizard man he wanted to wave to his father ~ not very likely really! She was similar to her sister ship the *Titanic*. The *Queen Mary* came into use in 1936 and with the large French *Normandie* (1935) carried many passengers to and fro.

The movements of these large ships were of great interest to us ~ they were so beautiful and each one had a distinguishing feature or two ~ we watched them come in from deep sea and in some cases they passed within a few miles of the coast. The Holland America Liner the *Statendam* with three yellow funnels with two green and one white band came so close that the band could be heard playing. Sadly she was destroyed by the Germans when Holland fell. After the war she was

The *Queen Mary* passing The Lizard inward bound from New York 1936 or later ~

photo J. Hart

92 THE LIZARD IN LANDEWEDNACK ~

replaced by the *Nieuw Amsterdam* the most beautiful of the ships we ever saw ~ she had two funnels and looked like a very large yacht. She was joined by two or three smaller ships and they continued on the Atlantic route until the jet aeroplanes took over. Then all went cruising from New York to the Caribbean.

We always saw Foreign ships nearer to the shore because they called at English ports before going to their home ports. Ours kept further out as they went to Cherbourg before ending the voyage at Southampton.

The German *Bremen* and the *Europa* both of the Nordduetscher Lloyd line were regularly seen in the 30s and in 1936 were supported by two large airships, the *Graf Zepplin* and the *Hindenburg*, which for a short time kept up a regular service, keeping outside the Lighthouse supposedly to prevent spying! The ships took five or six days to cross the Atlantic, so people in a hurry chose the airships, but after the disaster of the *Hindenburg* catching fire as she took up moorings on the masthead in Canada they were no longer used.

The *Queen Elizabeth* was not finished in time for a maiden voyage before the Second World War so in 1939 she dashed off to New York and in 1941 went on to Singapore where she was fitted out as a troopship. She and the *Queen Mary* carried thousands and thousands of troops throughout the war. They were so fast that they did not need an escort, and General Eisenhower thought their use had shortened the war. Finally they took thousands of G.Is home. Re-fitted they came back to the North Atlantic and continued till 1965/66. The *Queen Elizabeth* went to China and unfortunately was burnt out and destroyed and the *Queen Mary* is now a tourist attraction in America.

The United States line had several large ships which passed regularly. The *America* and the *United States* came to Plymouth and landed passengers by tender ~ so we saw them about three or four miles off ~ they had dark red funnels with a white ring below the black top. The *United States* took the Blue Riband from the *Queen Mary* which had held it for many years.

There were many other lines with smaller ships that we saw from time to time. The Union Castle Ships with lavender hulls, which went to South Africa, only passed when going for a re-fit. The distinctive colour of the hulls identified them easily. The ships going to South America did not come within sight of us either.

In about 1965 it was all change ~ the new ships being built were of a different design and looked strange. They still do! We had relied on the funnels for early recognition and they had altered from being tall and thin to being shorter and thicker; but still the number of funnels was the first thing to stand out when on the horizon. With the coming of the P.& O. liner *Canberra* the funnels went aft; others followed a similar design.

The flagship of the Cunard line, the *QE2*, only passes occasionally and is mostly cruising around the world. The new *Oriana* has just come into service having been built in Germany.

There are many other ships cruising but we seldom see them, and 'The Times' no longer prints 'Liners expected'.

Apart from the famous liners there were many ships of interest passing by ~ the British tankers being small by comparison with the enormous tankers we see on the horizon these days. The shape of these has changed ~ the bridge is no longer amidships and that makes it difficult to distinguish between tankers and bulk carriers.

There used to be a regular service ~ by small Coast line ships which carried cargoes and twelve passengers around the coast and they always called at Falmouth and had a depot there

~ and the Irish packets were very regular in their sailings too. Telescopes were kept at the ready and the ships' names were read by the one with the best eyesight! *Joan Hart*

~ THE GREAT LINERS ~

From Trethvas we had a grand view to the south and east of the diverse craft which passed coastwise or to and from North America. There were the Trans-Atlantic passenger and emigrant liners, flying the flags of France, Netherlands, U.S.A. and Britain, bearing names well-known in every household of the village.

I remember one still June evening the unmistakeable profile of the *Aquitania* appearing on the eastern horizon bound for New York. She was built in 1914, had survived two world wars and was now, in 1948, approaching the end of her very useful life. Originally burning coal but since converted to burn oil, she sported four enormous funnels venting copious quantities of black smoke which today would incur the wrath of conservationists the world over.

William Hocking

~ THE CHURCH COVE FISHING COMPANY ~ THE LIZARD ~

The Parish Council still pay £5 a year rent to the Trewithen Estate for the use of the slip at Church Cove by a few fishermen who still moor their boats in the Cove, enjoying fishing mainly for pleasure.

Documents held at The Record Office in Truro tell us that there was talk and plans to build a fish cellar in the Cove to market commercially the pilchards which at one time were caught in abundance by local fishermen.

However, it was not until 1837 that estimates and various plans were drawn up in earnest. The building was commissioned on behalf of C.H.J. Hawkins (a minor at the time, whose steward acted for him). In 1841 this was leased to a Mr Roskruge for a term of 15 years at a flat rate of £10 a year.

The Cellars again changed hands in 1856 to Foxes of Falmouth who complained in 1871 that repairs to the building and slip needed to be urgently attended to, and in 1872 it is recorded that they relinquished their lease. No further details exist in Truro, but from a book written by Cyril Noall 'Cornish Seines and Seiners' we learn further interesting details of that time. There is mention of the fact that 'The whole of the valuable concern called The Lizard Fishery was likewise auctioned at Helston on 26 June 1812. Included were three stop and one tuck seines, three seine boats, one carrying boat and two 'harkers', together with a large, almost new barking furnace and seine cabins'. So obviously a Company was in existence prior to 1837. Again he writes ~ 'The Lizard Fishery Establishment was mentioned in an advertisement dated 12 July 1828; it included a capstan house and slip, which gives it the command of the valuable stem of Kilcoben.

One later account reads as follows ~ '8 October 1879, on Friday morning at The Lizard pilchards appeared very early. In Lizard Cove a seine was shot and secured about 100 hogsheads.'

It is thought the Fishing Company ceased to function sometime after the First World War although it was not until the early 1930's that the Gulf Stream, having changed direction, drove the pilchards away from the Cornish coast. For the greater part of the period for which reliable records exist, the pilchard had been the principal species of fish caught in Cornish waters and the chief means of taking it was by the seine ~ an open net as opposed to the normal closed net. Shoals of pilchards provided a precarious living for the fisherman who was, like the Cornish miner, both a gambler and an optimist.

The fishing complex in Church Cove including a Winch and Capstan House was sold away from the Estate in 1947 to a Mr Charles Bosustow. For many years previous to that ~ apart from the 1939-45 war years when it had been wired off ~ various local fishermen had continued to use the buildings, but these and the slip had gradually fallen into disrepair. Mr Maitland, who aquired the property in 1949 was the first person to convert part of the complex into a private residence. He also blasted away the 'tail' of the slip ~ hoping to encourage the sand to enter the Cove. Of recent years the entire complex has been converted into separate homes.

Boats, cellars and winch-house at Church Cove ~

photo W. Hocking

The Season of 1878 ~

Bounty to Crew of Seiners in-lieu of Weekly Pay From 15 July to 24 December next ensuing.

£4	net money if the Crew secure from	40 ~ 50 Hogsheads of Pilchards
£5		50 ~ 60
£6		60 ~ 70
£7		70 ~ 80
£8		80 ~ 90
£9		90 ~ 100

£1 net for all over and above 100 Hogsheads of Pilchards, no matter what quantity may be secured over the 100 hogsheads in one Shoal.
The Seiners will also be paid day by day for securing such fish, boarding, drying, and housing seines, cordage, etc., and securing boats, etc., etc.
The Seiners will be entitled to one-quarter net profit arising from the sale of fish.
The Seiners as a Crew will divide the Bounty or Bounties amongst themselves as they may agree.
July 1878   *Derry Dobson*

CHAPTER THREE ~ THE SEA

~ HOUSEL BAY, BAY OF COMMUNICATIONS ~

To the immediate east of Lizard Head lies Housel Bay; a mere half mile across, yet whose unique position lent itself during the nineteenth and early twentieth centuries to the application of a variety of developing communication technologies particularly associated with ships but also in wider fields.

On the clifftop at the western end of the Bay stands the lighthouse. First lit in 1619 but then only for four years, it has now shone out for 243 years since it was rekindled in 1752 providing an optical communication to mariners, warning of the proximity of rocks and land and providing a welcome to those returning home.

A footpath winds along the cliff-edge from one end of the Bay to the other, proceeding as far as one pleases beyond it in each direction. Bumble Rock stands in the sea on proud guard at the western end, and at the eastern end are the heights of Pen Olver (or Penolver); at the centre of the Bay is Housel Cove, a very pleasant sandy beach.

Out at sea were ships trading with the countries of the world, leaving sight of land or carefully approaching it. Schemes were gradually invented and introduced in the Bay which aided their local navigation and communication and which were the forerunners of later world-wide systems.

The ship owners who sent out their ships, many months before in some cases, and with which they had since had no communication, would be keenly awaiting their return and would be anxious for their safety. They would wonder what cargoes they had and would want to make arrangements for their berthing, unloading and re-loading. One such company of ship owners and agents was G.C. Fox and Company of Falmouth, and this company was to make good use of the new electric telegraph which came to Falmouth in 1857. This electric telegraph, invented in the first half of the nineteenth century, provided a method of communications over land using electrical signals conveyed by wires hung from poles, the signals being in impulse form usually in accordance with the dots and dashes of the Morse code. The electric telegraph gradually spread between town and villages of the country, providing an enormous improvement in the speed of communication, as previously reliance was placed on messengers, horses and occasionally by optical means such as semaphore devices.

G.C. Fox and Company built a signalling station in 1872 at the eastern end of Housel Bay at Bass Point (once Beast Point) with road access to the village ~ the road now called Lloyd's Road. With this station, known as The Lizard Signal Station, the Company was able, in fine weather and with the aid of a recognised system of flag signals, to send messages to and from ships which were in sight of land. It was planned to bring the overland electric telegraph to the Station, but for a short period awaiting its installation the messages had to be carried by horse to the nearest telegraph station at Helston. Later in the same year, 1872, however, the Post Office completed the extension of the electric telegraph to the station and rooms were leased in the building by the Fox Company to the Post Office, the latter setting-up a telegraph office there and were responsible for sending and receiving the overland messages. Thus the Company was now able to convey messages in a short time not only between London and Falmouth but between Falmouth and ships off The Lizard, providing a very great increase in its efficiency of communication; information could now be received from the ships, and information and orders sent rapidly to them. Operation was extended to night time using lights, but was not possible in fog. The services were offered to other shipping companies and this became a very popular 24 hour operation, the telegraph office staying open at all times. This station thus provided a major step forward in maritime communication.

In 1883 part of the station was leased to Lloyd's who at that time had been setting up a number of signalling stations around the coast of the country and the station was then operated by Lloyd's with the telegraph still operated by the Post Office. The station became known as Lloyd's Signal Station. It continued in operation until 1951 by Lloyd's after which its operation of signalling and reporting was conducted by the coastguards on behalf of Lloyd's. Maritime signalling was discontinued in 1969. The building always announced itself with large lettering on its walls, and on its western and southern sides in the last century had the words V.R. Telegraph Office; later on the words on the western face were changed to Lloyd's Signal Station and it is these latter words by which the station has now become generally remembered. There were no mains water, sewage or power in those days, and all these services had to be self-provided; the remains of the precarious water source can be seen nearby part way down the cliff in Polledan Cove.

Operation of the station has on occasion unfortunately, led to the destruction of a ship. For instance in 1913 the 2144 ton four-masted barque *Queen Margaret*, 130 days out from Australia, signalled into the station and while waiting for final orders drifted onto the rocks and became a wreck.

The station building is still there on Bass Point and is now a residence leased from the National Trust who put it into good repair in 1994 and restored its exterior appearance to that of former times, even to the inclusion of the name of the station.

Whilst the electric telegraph was spreading extensively over land, it was being studied for undersea use to provide communication with countries overseas. By 1850 a submarine cable had been laid between England and France, and although it was only short-lived it was followed in a number of places by more reliable ones, and by 1866 even reliable trans-Atlantic cable operation was achieved. In 1872, almost as soon as Fox's signal station had been opened there were negotiations to bring a proposed cable from Bilbao in Spain into Housel Bay and terminate it in Fox's station. and so it was that in 1872 the cable was landed at the sandy beach at Housel Cove at the centre of the Bay, and an operating room was made available at the station. The Post Office with its overland telegraph then enabled messages to be transferred to their destinations with a minimum of delay. The company owning the cable is referred to in Kelly's directory of 1873 as the Bilbao (Spanish)

Lloyd's Signal Station and Telegraph Office prior to 1901 ~

photo J. Hart

CHAPTER THREE ~ THE SEA

1.—No. 116.

RECORD OF WIRELESS SIGNALS RECEIVED AT THE *Lizard* STATION.

18 . 4 . 10.

(Special Report 1651 Minnehaha = SOS Call)

Date and Time	From	To	Speed	Strength	Wave length in feet	Signal
Monday 18.4.10						
12.52 Am	MMA	LD	20	3	1600	Started sending Msg No 2 broke off suddenly says Std by and calls CQ CQ we may want help Std by SOS. SOS.
12.53	LD	MMA	·	—		K
12.54	MMA	LD				OK we may want help we have ground somewhere off Bishops on the Rocks - Stdby.
12.55	LD	MMA				OK if you have anything send it before JJ starts, pse send V's get best possible adjustment you are very weak can you give me better sigs.
Note: (Tried get Poldhu on land line to suspend programme few mins -)						
12.57	MMA	LD	·	3		Impossible in this weather NN Bits. (Note. Got best possible adjustment on Tune side sigs very weak.)
12.58	LD	MMA				OK Standing by.
12.59	"	SBA				please try get MAA on the Rocks off Bishop somewhere 1600 ft wave weak sigs I am jmd by JJ.
1.0	JJ	CQ				Started completely jmd MAA's adjustment
1.1	LD to Coastguard Stn and Lloyd's Sig Stn by Telephone.					"Minnehaha on the Rocks somewhere on Scilly's". Can we get thro' to Lifeboat Stn at Scilly via you or Lloyds, other than by Telegraph. Lloyd's & Cgds replied Telegraph Stns on Scilly closed but will get in touch with Falmouth and send tugs. No way getting thro' by us.
Note:						"Unable advise Lifeboat Stn at Scilly Office closed.

photo W. Hocking

Log of the first distress received at a British Coast Station by wireless telegraphy in 1910

Telegraph Company and in the book 'A Week at The Lizard' of 1883 the cable is called the Direct Spanish Electric Cable and it is this latter name which is usually applied. This cable can still be seen at the eastern side of the beach on its meandering track up the cliff face.

Whereas an overland telegraph cable suspended from insulators on poles was typically quite small in cross section, a cable to be laid on the sea bed had to have an insulation layer to insulate it from the sea and armoured layers outside to protect it from sea animals and from the motion of sea, sand and rocks. This made for an overall cable diameter of two inches. On the cliff it is let into a shallow trench and secured by iron cleats and protected by a layer of concrete. A cross section of the cable can be examined where it has fractured some way up the cliff. This cable operated successfully for several years, though the effects of wind and tide were considerable and led to some problems. In 1884 a new cable was laid into Kennack some four miles away where it was considered the local environment would be more favourable for the well-being of the cable. The cable into Housel Bay was taken out of service.

Thus we have seen the electric telegraph applied to overland and undersea communication, but ships still relied only on optical methods. This was all right for much of the time but was a complete failure in fog, and many shipwrecks occurred because the crews never saw land until it was too late to avoid hitting the rocks or cliffs. In 1878 the lighthouse added a new device ~ the foghorn ~ which at regular intervals blasted an audible signal out to sea in the hope that ships would be able on hearing it to be warned of the presence of of land and be able to determine an approximation of its direction and thus avoid impact with the coast. The benefit would seem to have been limited as shipwrecks in fog still continued at frequent intervals. It is surprising in retrospect that such acoustic devices were not developed into more useful systems as for instance might be achieved by using two spaced foghorns with triangulation at the ship providing an indication of location.

At the western side of the beach in Housel Cove a course of stonework can be seen above the sand and up the side of the cliff, and the purpose of this is not immediately obvious. However, at periods in the winter, and in some years more than others, when the tides have taken away the sand, a cable can be seen protruding from the base of the stonework. This too is an armoured underwater cable of two inch diameter, and was to operate a submerged bell off the headland below the foghorn. Each time the foghorn started to sound the bell was rung by an electrical signal through the underwater cable. The velocity of sound in water is different to that in air at 4950 and 1087 feet per second respectively, and thus the underwater bell signal would be heard at a ship before the foghorn. The interval between the received bell and foghorn signals gives a measure of distance from the shore at a scale of about four seconds per mile. Thus if the gap between the two signals is eight seconds then the coast is two miles away. For an interval of four seconds it is one mile away and for two seconds it is only half a mile away. It is believed that this system was installed at about the turn of the century but was not greatly used.

During the 1860s a mathematical physicist James Clerk Maxwell produced a theory that it would be possible to generate invisible electromagnetic waves that would radiate, and in 1888 an experimenter by the name of Heinrich Hertz announced that he had indeed produced such a radiation in his laboratory. A young Italian, Guglielmo Marconi, became aware of the experiments that were being made by a number of people in this field, and from 1894 he conducted his own experiments and developments. His achievements at first were, as for the other experimenters, with detection ranges of a few yards, but he soon drew ahead of the field and within a year he had extended detection to 1.5 miles. He was particularly interested in the possibilities of applying electro-magnetic waves to communication and almost from the start his equipment incorporated devices which could control transmissions according to the Morse code.

At this stage in 1896 Marconi came to work in England as he considered that he would be more likely to find support for his work there. He took as priority objectives the achievement of much longer operating ranges and the development of his equipment into practical wireless telegraphy communication equipment in order to be able to achieve the sales he sought. He found support in his work at first from the Post Office and over the next few years he made demonstrations to the Post Office, Army, Navy, Lloyd's, Trinity House and others as potential customers. In 1897 as a result of his developments the range had increased to 4.5 miles, in 1898 to 14.5 miles, in 1899 to 32 miles across the English Channel and to 87 miles in naval and other demonstrations. Whilst Marconi was not alone in wireless development he consistently achieved better results than others.

Operation out to about 80 miles might seem to be a very successful achievement, but there were problems when a number of stations operated at the same time, for the circuits in which the spark transmitters and coherer detectors were configured were such that all stations interfered with the others, and by 1900 the only customer had been the Navy. In addition Marconi was advised most strongly by many scientific people of the time that his system would never work beyond the horizon whereas Marconi believed it would. Marconi did three things to overcome these problems. Firstly he developed 'jiggers' or tuned circuits to include in his equipment whereby each transmitter/receiver could be tuned to its own frequency thus allowing several stations to operate at the same time. Secondly to assist the introduction of equipment he leased transmitter/receiver wireless telegraphy sets to ships of any nationality and in 1900 and 1901 built seven shore stations on the coast for communicating with this equipment on the ships. Thirdly to prove that very long range transmission was possible he planned to build a large transmitting station at Poldhu in Cornwall and to endeavour to detect its transmissions at the other side of the Atlantic ocean.

It was at this time that Marconi came to The Lizard and set up The Lizard Wireless station in Housel Bay to assist in furthering the work outlined above. The station had three purposes. Firstly to test the transmissions of the nearby Poldhu Station during its development some six miles away. Secondly to test the capability of tuned circuits to permit successful operation in the proximity of a powerful station and thirdly as an additional wireless telegraphy station for ship to shore operation. On 23 January 1901 a new record for wireless communication of 186 miles was set up between The Lizard and Isle of Wight Stations. The horizon from the top of Marconi's mast was 18 miles and thus two masts of this height would just be visible to each other at 36 miles; the achievement of a wireless range of over five times this was therefore a major milestone in his quest for long range operation and a great encouragement to him that his vision of over-the-horizon operation was possible, and indeed was described by some at the time as the first of his two great miracles. The second miracle was to take place later in the year in December from Poldhu, when its signals were received on the other side of the Atlantic ocean.

The Lizard Wireless Station was contained in a two-roomed wooden hut which housed a ten inch induction coil transmitter and a coherer receiver with power provided by a battery of cells. A second hut provided accommodation for the operators. At a later date the battery was replaced by accumulators charged by a dynamo driven from an engine.

The station was therefore busy during the early developments at Poldhu and became ever more busy on ship to shore traffic as more and more ships introduced wireless equipment. It continued as a Marconi Station until 1908 when the Post Office became responsible for its operation, albeit with Marconi staff assistance until 1911. The station was closed in 1913 when the new Land's End radio station started operations, but was reopened during the First World War and closed finally in 1920 when the equipment and aerial were dismantled. A bronze plaque erected by the Marconi Company in 1953 records Marconi's work there ~ 'Guglielmo Marconi whose pioneer work in wireless telegraphy for the safety of all seafarers was furthered in this building during the first years of the century'. The buildings used are still there on the cliff top about midway between the beach and Lloyd's Signal Station and are presently a private residence. There is a further reminder of Marconi in the Bay as one of the houses overlooking the sea used timber in its constructions from Poldhu Station when it was dismantled.

Thus over a period of 30 years in the Bay at the end of the nineteenth and the beginning of the twentieth centuries a wide range of communication systems had been used following on from the much earlier optical signals from the lighthouse. To these had been added clear weather optical message signalling with ships to and from the Fox's/Lloyd's Signal Station by flags and lights, the electrical telegraph over land to Fox's Signal Station, the electrical telegraph under sea to Spain using submarine cables, airborne and underwater sound warnings in fog by the foghorn and underwater bell, and then wireless telegraphy operation by The Lizard Wireless Station which at last achieved all-weather communication with ships. Since 1900 the applications of wireless communication and navigation have increased enormously and especially during and since the First World War, and modern developments have made all but the lighthouse and foghorn obsolete. One hears rumblings that even these may one day not be needed. It is particularly interesting that there is still evidence of all the systems either in the form of buildings or cables though the Lloyd's, Marconi and cable equipment has long since gone. It is encouraging that the National Trust has ensured that the Lloyd's Signal Station building will survive and be maintained; perhaps if the lighthouse should ever close then this time the buildings and equipment will be retained for future generations to see what once was here.

The Lighthouse and Lloyd's Signal Station are now listed in the National Monuments Record as historic monuments, and that body holds descriptive summaries and photographs of the buildings. *Courtney Rowe*

CHAPTER FOUR

Memories & Family Businesses

~ IF ONLY WALLS COULD TALK ~

'If only walls could talk'. So runs one of the comments written by a visitor to Landewednack Church in the Visitor's Book that lay open from 22 June 1993 to 6 September 1995. Such volumes are peculiar to churches, royal palaces and some other public buildings which visitors are wont to enter.

Why do people who come to a place like The Lizard include the parish church on their itinerary? What do those who make entries in the Visitor's Book there intend by doing so? The answers may not be as straightforward as might be thought, unlike the heavily incised, large lettered, 'Well worth a visit'. Straightforward and down to earth but hardly revealing.

Language can be a problem. Some make what may be carefully thought out comments, but in an unfamiliar language. 'If walls could talk' how much more might be known about the impression St Wynwallow's made upon ~ was it a German speaker with limited English, who none the less had the courtesy to write, 'very interesting'?

Not a few entries are what might be called impartial, the individual apparently unaffected by entering a consecrated building. Others come seeking sanctuary, grateful to be welcomed by 'serene tranquillity and silence', pleased at the well kept state of the building, and the pews 'the most comfortable I have ever sat in', (although in one case remarking, 'peaceful, but regret masonry techniques used!'). Flower arrangers are rewarded for their labours; visitors are enchanted by the display and fragrance of the flowers.

Gratitude. There are those who express their gratitude for a place, as one visitor to Landewednack put it, 'to find oneself'. Another entry says briefly, 'atmospherical'. A 'gentler scribe' found 'warm silence', and a Canadian something too often lacking in our clamourous society, 'a quality of joy'. Others set out from wherever to reach the church ~ 'lovely to reach here' (although he or she ventured from no further away than Newquay). Some come for baptisms, weddings, funerals. Couples traverse land and sea from as far away as the Antipodes, or, nearer home, the Isle of Man ~ 'Thank you for our wedding'. The ones from New Zealand returned to 'celebrate our twenty-fifth wedding anniversary'; another couple recalled their wedding many years before. Some express future hope ~ 'I want to be married here'. It may be wondered how many marriages have been saved and families reunited because the couples have 'come apart and rested a while' from 'the strife of tongues' to find reconciliation in a church with an open door. 'Fightings within and fears without' may refer to inner turmoil and marital conflict as much as to the battle of wind and weather. Situated where it is, the church is often a shelter from the wind and rain ~ 'very windy weather outside, but peaceful inside', or 'peaceful and relaxing contrast to the windswept coast'.

From New Zealand came a visitor who stayed with Charlie Roberts in 1940 when he came to The Lizard as an evacuee from London. He, who was sent here through the fortunes of war, now sought Cornwall as a place to return to. Perhaps he, all those years ago, was walking off a Christmas Day lunch when a German warship hove in sight off Bass Point, coming close enough for the crew to wave to whoever was on duty in the Lookout.

Come and See. Some come from far and near to remember their ancestors ~ 'Come to see our forefathers in the graveyard'. For those who go down into Church Cove or to Kilcobben and stand looking out to sea there are names evocative of past tragedies ~ 'Come to see the grave of the wireless operator of the *S.S.Gairsoppa*'. Was the visitor a relative? It is not written. The descendants of Goodman, The Lizard blacksmith, came to remember him.

Hostel Accommodation. One visitor turns up every two or three months. With large, darkly inked letters he describes himself as 'Commercial driver by trade and long distance walker'. Had his lorry broken down, or had he tramped over cliff and through cove? On one occasion, over the bottom line of one page and across the top of the next, he records his birth in Oxford and his present abode in Plymouth and adds, 'I found rest and peace here last night by sleeping outside in the church porch on the coconut mats'. He must have been tired for he does not mention being troubled by the martins who have reared their young in a nest built above one of the bosses in the arch of the porch. They provided welcome for others who wrote, 'beautiful and tranquil. We were welcomed by the swallows'. Contrarily some one else, who may have saved the coconut matting from yet another liming, wrote crossly, 'You need to get rid of that nest'.

Practical Request. A Visitor's Book does not often prompt a written response to action request. Was the visit specific or a chance one, for a relative, one assumes, to ask for the restoration of 'the last name on the Great War memorial in the north-west aisle wall'? A marginal note confirms, 'Yes, now done, 27.10.93'.

One was helped ~ 'lovely to light a candle'. Perhaps so too was the agonised teenager, 'Exam results today ~ don't let my Dad shout at me. Thank God'. Was the thanksgiving added later? Further entries testify to grace given: 'the strength I needed', 'healing and generous', 'the gentle feeling of safety', while for yet others a means of 're-finding childhood roots' or providing 'a great oasis in a troubled world'.

Pilgrim Way. Groups of people look in from time to time, some to pray, others to stand and stare. Among the prayerful are those who describe themselves as pilgrims ~ 'A Celtic Pilgrimage' or as members of Christian groups ~ 'a cycle ride for Romania'. Some come with local concerns: 'We enter this church with thoughts of the lifeboatmen'.

Something Overheard. Comments about the bells are laudatory, both at hearing them and being allowed to watch the band of ringers. Latin and Japanese as well as European languages appear; choruses from song books are quoted; young visitors illuminate their entries. Miranda, aged 10, draws an angel, which must be said, looks less aerodynamic than a Sea King helicopter; elsewhere are decorative crosses, along with, less predictably, hearts and kisses. 'God will like it here'. It is to be hoped he does!

'If walls could talk' perhaps revealed would be the unwritten, unspoken response to the holy place, rather than just another stop-over place in the tourists' itinerary. Whoever they are, the church elicits superlatives that belie its modest stones. Those who know it are happy at returning 'always a joy to visit'. So even though you may not hear 'a lovely ringing of bells' as did a grateful Swede, raise the latch. It is very old and somewhat stiff ~ push open the door, pray if needs be 'for a dear friend', and for all who worship here for, surely, 'The Lord is in this place ...'

J.R.H.P.

CHAPTER FOUR ~ MEMORIES AND FAMILY BUSINESSES

~ THE LIZARD ~ THE WAR YEARS ~

Coastguards ~

There were two Coastguards Stations. The summer-house from Tresawle was re-erected on Kattan Point and became Lizard East. Lizard West was The Lizard Head Station. The Coastguard regulars were Mr. Phillips ~ Station Officer, Mr. Legge and George French; Auxiliaries were Benny Bosustow, Howard Mitchell, Yeo Williams, Fred Harris, Herbert Pascoe and Larry Olivey.

The Home Guard ~

The Home Guard (or Local Defence Volunteers as they were originally called) was worse than 'Dad's Army' when they were first formed. They were given arm bands with LDV on them and were armed with anything they could pick up ~ swords, pitch forks and broom handles. They kept watch on top of Lloyds Signal Station. Later they were better armed and had a rifle range down at the quarry below the Signal Station. On incident in particular I remember ~ Alfie Dick being shot in the eye by a blank cartridge.

Army Cadets ~

Lofty Richards and I who were only eleven years old added twelve months to our age so we could join. The first weapons we had were single shot French carbines and then Short Lee Enfield rifles. The public would have a fit if they saw eleven year olds running round the village with real live rifles today! The headquarters for both the Home Guard and the Army Cadets was in Hill's tea rooms.

The following buildings were commandeered later on in the war, although most of them started out as evacuee hostels. The two big houses opposite Parc-an-Castle main gates, Colonel Semple's House, Rocklands, half of Hill's Hotel and half of Kynance Bay Hotel, Tresawle, Morwenna, Butcher's House, Penolver Cottages, Henry Dennis' bungalow and Marconi's (Mrs Kempthorn's). Housel Bay Hotel was entirely RAF as were Penolver Cottages.

I used to live in Penolver Cottages until they were commandeered. Mrs Wilks' next door was turned into a sickbay, while the front room downstairs was the guard room and the back kitchen was the armoury. There were three gun pits dug, with twin Lewis guns in each. One of the airmen married the Vicar's daughter. At Bass Point the Lloyds Signal Station night box was taken over by the RAF and was moved to the building below. In the early part of the war there were many evacuees in the village. The family who came to live in Henry Dennis' bungalow arrived in the dark and when they got up the next morning and saw the sea they remarked how big the pool was ~ never having seen the sea before!

The Americans were here too ~ the 29th and 35th Divisions. If you were to look carefully on the wall in the Reading Room you might still be able to see the 29th Division crest which was painted on the wall leading to the back rooms.

Several incidents come to my mind. There was a French family who escaped across the Channel and Dick Roberts went out and guided their boat into Polpeor. The grateful French gave their boat to Dick but the next day a ML from Falmouth took it out to sea and sank it! Another time a ML ran aground on Parnvoose beach. I was going down to have a look at it, but was caught by my mother before I had got far. As for bombs ~ there were five at least, possibly six. There were two big ones and I would say four small ones, one of which did not explode and was taken away on a lorry. The small bombs dropped on Stevens' farm land. We use to wave to a Sunderland flying boat which flew over Bass Point every day, and they would wave back.

When I used to live down at Lloyds the only other children there were Neville Green and Gloria Barrett, but as I was older I used to stay up in the village and play. I would ask the sentry what the password was in case I came back in the dark. He would say something like 'Tripe and Onions'. On occasions I would forget what the password was. When challenged I would say, 'You know who I am' but while he kept me talking the other guard would creep up behind me, and taking me by the scruff of the neck would march me into the guard room. As the walls between the houses were quite thin my mother could hear me being questioned. From our back bedroom window Anne and I used to watch the raids on Falmouth Docks and see the search lights and the bursts of anti-aircraft fire.

The Little Ship on the Green (where Jimmy Hill used to live) was the local Dance Hall and cinema. When a dance was held the cakes etc. were supplied by Charlie Wearnes of Helston and we used to try and sneak in at the back and steal them. We also used the same methods to see the local cinema shows. As Army Cadets we used to put on our uniforms and go up to the airfield for coffee and slab cake, or play ping-pong in the YMCA or go to the NAAFI for Walls ice cream. We could also use the camp cinema and would think nothing of walking there and back in the dark, or of the 'bad' welcome we would get on our arrival home!

Servicemen from the village who returned home from the war ~

Army ~ Bert Pascoe, Arly Richards, Phil Burgess, Leslie Hendy, Pat Bosustow, Robin Bosustow & Mr Francis.

Navy ~ Douglas Mitchell, Johnny Belman, Wilfred Harris, Dickie Roberts, Raymond Hendy, Arthur Johns, Reggie Johns, Sweeny Todd, Ivan Tyack, Jackie Tyack, Eric Mitchell, Dumps Johnson, Lloyd Johnson, Frank Johnson & Peter Mitchell.

RAF ~ Cecil Bray, Arthur Matthews, Roger Richards, Norman Bray, Franklyn Roberts, Whiskey Johns, Tangye Cox & Billy Casley.

Merchant Navy ~ Jimmy Hill & Alex Hill.

John Bosustow

~ PENMENNER HOUSE LOCK-UP ~

Before the First World War Penmenner House was the favoured holiday home of Virginia Woolf, Oscar Wilde and Rupert Brooke; in the Second World War its basement provided a secure lock-up facility. At one point in time an American airman having committed a murder at near-by Predannack Airfield was charged and held in custody in this makeshift cell, prior to being taken up-country by the military police. *Brian Richards*

CHAPTER FOUR ~ MEMORIES & FAMILY BUSINESSES

~ WARTIME MEMORIES ~

At the outbreak of war I was in my mid-teens and at an impressionable age. My memories of the war are very strong.

In 1940 the Germans occupied airfields in northern France and were then only 20 minutes flying time from targets in south-west England. One morning a lone cyclist could be seen pedalling along Penmenner Road where I then lived. He wore a 'tin hat', had a gas mask slung from his shoulder and we could hear the short sharp blasts he blew on his whistle. It was Percy Emmott, the A.R.P. warden, and we were supposed to take cover. I cannot remember any subsequent warnings, but in 1940 we all felt threatened. A military airfield was under construction at Predannack and a powerful radar station at Bass Point. The latter was once attacked, although the bombs fell harmlessly into one of Tom Hendy's fields.

The second event was later that year. I am sure it was Sunday morning 24 November, and chapel services were over, people had bought their Sunday newspapers from Mr Mundy and the village had its usual deserted look for that time of the week. From my home I heard the sound of aircraft, but also the distinctive rattle of machine guns. I rushed outside to see two Spitfires attacking a German bomber. The enemy aircraft was quite low and seemed unable to maintain its height. Each Spitfire attacked in turn, diving from above and at such an angle as might lessen the possibility of return fire. I soon lost sight of the German plane, and when two British planes did their victory rolls I assumed the German bomber had fallen into the sea somewhere off Lizard Head. Later that day the lifeboat brought ashore the one survivor. He was rested in a bungalow overlooking Polpeor Cove. I have sometimes wondered if the relatives of those who died in that Dornier bomber have ever visited our village and looked seaward from Lizard Head to the crew's final resting place.

In 1944 I began my training for aircraft duties, but my final course in Canada came to an abrupt end when Japan surrendered. *Des Holden*

~ CARMELLIN CROFT ~

Carmellin Croft, so named for over 200 years, belonged to an architect, Robert Collier, at the turn of the century when the house now known as Carmellin Croft was built. In 1929 Colonel the Master of Semple and his family came to The Lizard and rented the house. During that time Lord Semple, as he became, was in 'business' and came and went, but Lady Semple and their two daughters lived there until 1939. Just before the outbreak of war Lady Semple died and the younger daughter, June, was later killed in the London Blitz. The eldest daughter is now the Countess of Semple, having inherited her father's Scottish title. Lord Semple himself remarried and had four more daughters. He last visited the village in 1967 about which time Carmellin was sold for £2,500 by the Collier family.

Lord Semple had a wide circle of German acquaintances and his two eldest daughters were educated in Germany before the war. Both Rippentrop and Goering visited the family frequently in the 1930s. The Emperor Hirohito of Japan was also a visitor to Carmellin. A number of flying enthusiasts, both British and German, were among Lord Semple's friends, for he owned his own aeroplane and used a large field which he rented, as a private landing strip. *Derry Dobson*

~ THE TRAGIC LOSS OF THE GAIRSOPPA ~

Near the stile at the lower end of Landewednack churchyard amid the lichen-crusted slate and granite memorials lies a headstone as clean and pristine as the day it was erected. This war grave memorial reads: 'R.F.Hampshire, Radio Officer, S.S.Gairsoppa, 16 February 1941'. Behind this terse inscription lies a story as sad as any to emerge from a conflict where human tragedy knew no bounds.

The story concerns the British India Steam Navigation Steamship *Gairsoppa* and her crew of 85 comprising 15 Europeans and 70 Indians. She measured 5,237 tonnes gross, was coal-fired and carried a cargo of pig iron. At the and of January 1941 she left Freetown, West Africa, in convoy SL64 bound for the United Kingdom. By 14th February bunkers were running desperately low and it was decided that she should reduce speed to 5 knots and set course for the nearest safe port. She no longer enjoyed the relative safety of the convoy.

Two days later, on the 16th, when approximately 300 miles southwest of Galway she was shadowed by a German reconnaissance aircraft. At about 10.30pm that night a torpedo fired by submarine U101 struck the vessel forward on the starboard side. Under very difficult circumstances, high seas, darkness and a listing ship, the crew succeeded in launching three of the four lifeboats. Two were not seen again.

About thirty crew got away in the third lifeboat under command of the Second Officer. Basic protection was provided by the erection of canvas shelters, the sail hoisted and limited control of the rudderless craft maintained by an oar. The harsh North Atlantic winter took its toll of the hapless survivors. Daily more and more succumbed until on the 13th day only the Radio Officer, a seaman gunner and the Second Officer remained alive. On sighting the Lighthouse and the hostile shore of Landewednack they were too weak to do more than reduce sail. They were driven inexorably towards the surf of Caerthillian Cove.

Their plight was seen by motor-mechanic, William Stephens, who raised the alarm but before The Lizard Lifeboat could reach them, their boat had capsized and all were thrown into the raging surf. Only the second officer was pulled from the sea alive.

Radio officer Robert Frederick Hampshire lies near one of his shipmates, Norman Thomas and an unknown Indian seaman, in the peace and quiet of Landewednack churchyard. He died on 1 March 1941 aged 18. *William Hocking*

~ GROUP-CAPTAIN LEONARD CHESHIRE ~

At 27, Leonard Cheshire witnessed the explosion of the second atomic bomb on Nagasaki, which was to bring about the end of the first global war ~ a war in which he had piloted a hundred missions over enemy Europe and received three D.S.O.s, a D.F.C. and a Victoria Cross.

He came out of the R.A.F. in 1946, burnt-out and exhausted but with the first seeds of an idea and the burning conviction, which was never to leave him, that the world must, to survive, turn to a Christian way of life ~ the killing of humanity by humanity had to end.

The first seeds died, but the idea was right: and undeterred by initial failure he set up his first Home ~ 'Le Court' in Hampshire ~ where people who were sick, disabled and unwanted could live out their lives in dignity, surrounded by care and kindness.

CHAPTER FOUR ~ MEMORIES AND FAMILY BUSINESSES

The need for such 'Homes' was obviously there as a few years later, in 1951, whilst working with Barnes Wallis for Vicker's Armstrong's research team, St Teresa's and Holy Cross (Cheshire's second and third Homes) found temporary accommodation in a group of disused nissan huts on the edge of Predannack Airfield. The buildings were converted into a livable state by largely voluntary help from the Vicker's Armstrong staff, men from H.M.S. Seahawk (Culdrose servicemen) and locals from the surrounding villages of Mullion, Ruan Minor and The Lizard. The project was initially financed on a shoestring budget. By 1953 however, the Carnegie Trust had become involved and bigger and better surroundings at Marazion were found. Cheshire himself became very ill with T.B. and had to be hospitalised, but this did not stop him campaigning for funds and publicity.

Throughout the rest of his life Leonard Cheshire never lost sight of his original idea ~ to provide homes for those in need no matter what their colour, creed or state of health. Internationally the Cheshire Foundation Homes are well-known to all, but locally, it is St Teresa's as it was in the early 'struggling' days that is remembered most clearly ~ that and the image of a gaunt young/old man with unflagging energy and a winning smile. *Derry Dobson*

~ MEMORIES OF A CORNISH CHILDHOOD ~

I was barely a year old when W.W.2 broke out so I was blissfully unaware of what this entailed. At that time we lived down by Lloyd's Signal Station at Penolver Cottage. My earliest recollections are of going down the cliff with my father to get water from a well. Some mornings we would wave to the crew of the Sunderland flying boat which came over so low that we could actually see the men. Occasionally it would land on the sea and make contact with Lloyd's.

When I was three we moved into Belsize Cottage and my sister Judy was born. I remember that morning well. My brother John and I were shut in a bedroom totally ignorant of what was happening. On hearing the new arrival's cries we wanted to be let out so that we could see 'Farmer Richard's piglets!'

One day going along the Beacon with my mother the air raid siren sounded. Mrs Emmott was in the garden and asked us into her house ~ everyone had to be under cover. The two women sat at a table drinking tea whilst Gill, Judy and I were sheltering underneath from the bombs which never came! However, on another occasion I remember seeing the skies towards Church Cove were glowing red like a tropical sunset and Mother told me it was Falmouth burning after being bombed. John and I often used to watch the searchlights sweeping the skies. My Father, being too old to join up, was in the Coastguards ~ he used to do a night shift and came home in the small hours ~ climbing through the kitchen window because the door was locked when the rest of the family was abed! His rifles was always propped up in a corner of the kitchen when he was off duty.

Everyone had to do their bit for the war effort. Newspaper and cardboard was saved in all households and the children went around the doors collecting 'salvage' as it was called. John and I would go up the road to Mrs Jenner but as we rounded the bend in her drive I used to think that Mrs Jenner was always waiting for us outside the front door. This unnerved me and I wouldn't go any farther, so John went on alone. Eventually I was persuaded to go with him and I met Lady Dufferin, a ship's figurehead that stood beside the front door.

I remember starting school in the Reading Room. Miss Underwood was my teacher. How many people recall doing 'picking' ~ pulling threads out of cotton material ~ to make a sort of coarse cotton wool? I think it was cotton waste used for cleaning guns but I can't be sure. Then we moved into the school. Every morning began with a hymn and a prayer. Sometimes there were three classes and sometimes four, depending on the number of children attending the school. Those were the days when one could not complete one's education without changing schools. If you passed the 'Eleven Plus' you went to Helston Grammar School, catching the service bus at eight o'clock and returning home at five.

Those children who had not passed, stayed on until they left at fourteen. Later the leaving age was raised to fifteen. Mr Lawrence was the headmaster when I started, then Mr Warren who lived down Caerthillian Road.

Oh, the Christmas concerts we had! One year the top class performed 'A Christmas Carol'. I was enchanted and I'll never forget it. The final night they had a *real* chicken *and* Christmas pudding! Then there was the Christmas Carol Service and party to look forward to with great excitement.

The older boys tended the school gardens over at Cross Common, growing vegetables and soft fruits ~ skills to last a lifetime were learnt there. The senior girls were taught sewing ~ they each made a blouse with a yoke, puffed sleeves and a Peter Pan collar which when completed and worn would make a stick insect look like a buxom wench! They also made knickers with wide legs, a waistband and side placket in pastel lawn material.

Sport was encouraged. In the summer it was rounders for girls ~ cricket for the boys. Come winter, the girls played netball, the boys football. The school teams competed against other schools and two years running the boys' football team reached the final of the Perry Cup. This took place over at Mullion and a coach was hired to take supporters to cheer them on. At half-time we went to the Chip shop ~ a rare treat. The first year the boys lost and there was great disappointment; the second, they won after extra time and we all went back to the school and drank blackcurrant juice out of the cup. What a celebration!

Good attendance at school was encouraged by way of an 'Attendance Banner'. It was made of red satin in a shield shape with gold braid and tassels and embroidered with the words 'Best attendance this Week'. The class with the best attendance was allowed to hang this banner in the classroom. One week the infants had one hundred percent attendance until the Friday afternoon when Judy and Pilchard went missing. They had wandered off down to Housel Bay to pick bluebells! There was more fuss made over the loss of that banner for a week than there was over the two missing children. The two Johns were sent to find the truants who were duly punished. The school day always ended as it began with a hymn and a prayer.

Most people practised religion ~ one was either Church or Chapel. I used to go to Church three times on Sundays ~ Matins, Sunday School and Evensong. We were anything but angels ~ before Sunday School we'd climb over the churchyard wall into the Rector's orchard, scrump his apples and eat them in Church. We thought at the time that he didn't know where these apples came from. In the Rev. Barratt's day the Annual Sunday School outing was always to Kennack Sands but we didn't go onto the beach ~ we always went up to the woods behind. We were taken there in a trailer with forms for seating ~ courtesy of Hedley Stevens' Dad. I believe the trailer was hitched to a tractor. Food was transported in big wicker baskets lined with white cloths. There were splits and yeast buns and fruit cake. We went up to a glade and whilst the

CHAPTER FOUR ~ MEMORIES & FAMILY BUSINESSES

adults prepared the picnic, the children explored the woods, going over the stream and looking at the sea defences. I think it was after Rev. Frederick Simpson came that we started going to St Ives in a coach. We took our packed lunches and ate them on the beach. For most children the highlight of the day was the train ride to Carbis Bay ~ I know it was for me; that, and the Laughing Sailor in the Amusement Arcade. We'd have our tea in a café up steps overlooking the beach and usually ended the day with a bag of chips before we returned home tired out. Happy days to remember.

Come the teenage years, we joined the Youth Club run by Miss Perry, Miss Smitherham and then by Florence Lyne. There we played table tennis and board games or learnt to dance to records. We had a Birthday Bash each year. When it was my age group's turn to organise this we scrounged the basic ingredients from our parents and then spent the whole weekend baking sausage rolls and fairy cakes and suchlike. The party was always on a Monday and as many as possible left school and work early to get the room ready and lay up the tables. We usually hired a band ~ either the 'Blue Aces' or 'Clavatone' and invited St Keverne and Coverack Youth Clubs to join us. The only drinks available were orange and lemon squash ~ alcohol was unheard of at such a do, but a good time was had by all. How the times have changed since the fifties!

My first visit to the pictures was in the Old Chapel on the Green, but mostly I remember going to the Reading Room where Mr Barber came with his van once a week in winter, twice a week in summer. The cheapest seats were on the forms in the front row, and the dearest on chairs at the back. You could bring your own cushion or hire one for a few pence. Girls were separated from the boys and if there was any noise or disruption the lights went up. By present day standards we had good value for our money. There was the Pathé Newsreel, a serial, a 'B' film, the trailer for next week's film and finally the feature film. During the interval one could buy ice cream and cartons of squash.

When we weren't in Church or at the Youth Club we spent hours exploring the cliffs and the beaches. Mrs Jenner had a marvellous old book about The Lizard which she let me read and Amy, Derry and I would follow it up. One day we were the Pystyll side of Polpeor 'investigating' a cave. Bob Mitchell was on the beach digging bait. The three of us clambered over a great pile of seaweed into a cave. At first it was quite dark but when we grew accustomed to it we ventured farther in. There in the back of the cave was this white apparition. We scarpered back out to the seaweed, onto the beach screaming to Bob that there was a skeleton in the cave. Bob left his digging and over the seaweed he went and into the cave. When he reappeared he shouted 'Here's your bloody skeleton', and held aloft a cabbage stalk that had sprouted in the dark!

One summer the older boys made a raft of oildrums lashed together with ropes. About half a dozen of us went to sea on it each straddling an oildrum. We had a couple of paddles and went quite a way out and had a wonderful time. When we came back into Polpeor the cliffs were lined with people watching us all; apparently someone had considered calling out the lifeboat! We were completely unaware of any dangers and had thoroughly enjoyed ourselves. If we felt like a good swim we would go to Shag Rock and back. Winter or summer there was always plenty of interest on the beach or around the cliffs, and we were never bored.

I wonder how many people remember the 'old timers' of our youth who so unwittingly enriched our lives. There was Fanny Toy who kept bees in the back garden. She always told them what was going on! I loved her fresh crusts with honey. Then there was Mrs Jose ~ we'd go into her house and she'd let us play with her 'peckitty bird'. This was clockwork, and pecked at the tablecloth. She also allowed us to lay and light the fire using a set of bellows. We'd pump the bellows and fill the house with smoke. Bertha Willy often came into our house at night and told us ghost stories. Judy and I would be too frightened to go to bed but we still liked to listen. There was an old man I can remember, who had a long, long beard, I used to meet him along the Beacon on a Sunday after Sunday School. He always had a staff in his hand and I suppose because of his appearance he looked somewhat biblical. I thought he was God! I used to feel quite overwhelmed.

I remember going next door to Granny Johns and having to sing or recite and getting sweets in return on Shrove Tuesday. This was 'Colperra'. I suppose it was like 'Trick or Treat' of today.

These are just a few of my memories of growing up in The Lizard.

Anne Bosustow ~ now Tyler.

~ THE ANCIENT CUSTOM OF COLPERRA ~

Until the 1950's, when sadly it finally died out, Colperra had been a yearly custom specific to no other village than The Lizard. On Shrove Tuesday ~ the day before the beginning of Lent ~ all the village children would have time off morning school to go from house to house collecting 'excess' food. Parkin especially made with treacle was reputedly cooked, anticipating the children's arrival ~ eggs, oranges and pennies were also favoured items for collection.

It's uncertain how this ancient custom came into existence but one suggestion has been that it was a feasible way of collecting food for shipwrecked sailors. *Freda Lawrence*

~ THE WITCHBALL RESTAURANT ~

Situated a hundred yards from the village green, on the road leading to the Lighthouse and Lizard Point stands the Witchball Restaurant, one of the oldest buildings on The Lizard. When we were in the process of buying it some ten years ago our surveyor's report said that it was about 400 years old, putting it at about the time of the Spanish Armada. Previously called Alma Farm, many people still living in The Lizard have connections with this old building.

The building itself is made of stone and cob and still has parts of the old scantle slate roof of which there are very few left. This one unfortunately, due to the ravages of time, will soon have to be renewed. The roof timbers are old ships' timbers from local shipwrecks. We have our own well in the front garden, although it is now concealed beneath a slate slab. The restaurant is one large L-shaped room made out of what were originally three family rooms. There is still a door catch hidden behind one old timber. For many years it was a working farm and at one time the kitchen was a piggery and the bedrooms were above a hayloft. The front part of the house was a coach house.

Needless to say, being such an old building, it is haunted and has a resident ghost or two. It is said that a groom when attending a horse in the coach house was kicked in the head and killed. He now enjoys moving objects and hiding them, then replacing them which is not always amusing. At Christmas 1994 we had a medium from London dining and after she had finished her meal she asked if we had anything to do with the Spanish as she had seen an ancient Spanish soldier standing in a corner of the room. She emphasised however that he was a very friendly ghost.

Barbara Hampshire.

CHAPTER FOUR ~ MEMORIES & FAMILY BUSINESSES

~ HENDY'S GIFT SHOP ~

This shop was originally a Cart House for Alma Farm ~ now the Witchball Restaurant. At some time in the past this property was owned by the Hendy family. The Cart House was turned into a Serpentine shop by Raymond Hendy in 1947. The meadow beside it, where now stands a bungalow, was once part of Trenoweth Farm and used by Hill's Hotel as a vegetable garden.

John Hendy

~ MARTHA'S WELL CREASE ~

Today, we know it as 'The Top House' the friendly village pub. 200 years ago however, the building was already in existence, but as a farm with the fascinating name of 'Martha's Well Crease'. (There is a closed off well to the right of the main entrance).

Records show that it was leased and worked by the Hill family for some time prior to their buying it in 1799 for 5/- and 9 Peppercorns. The census of 1841 tells us that three generations of Hills were in residence at that point in time. It would have been about 1870 when the farmhouse opened its doors to its first visitors ~ seasonal tourists were already discovering the delights of a Cornish Holiday! Hill's Hotel, as it was renamed, gradually ceased to be a working farm, and additional residential accommodation was built in the mowhay behind the farm-house.

The property remained in the Hill family until 1950 when it was sold to the Devenish Brewery. A Mr Greenslade took over the tenancy ~ his son Peter being the present Landlord.

~ J.A.R. HILL SERPENTINE AND GIFT SHOP ~

This building in the square has had a long and varied career. Originally the horse stable for Martha's Well Crease Farm, it was then used to stable the Coach horses travelling to and from Helston. When motorised buses arrived on the scene however, the stable was converted into a tea-room being an extension to 'Hill's Hotel' opposite. During the war years it did duty as an exercise and meeting room for the Home Guard and finally in the late 40's it was transformed into the Serpentine Shop we now see.

Many people remember the pump and granite water trough which used to be on the corner just behind the shop ~ there for the convenience of the horses! *David Hill*

~ THE FIRST MOTORISED BUS SERVICE ~

93 years ago, on the 17th, August 1903, history was made when 22 people seated themselves in a Milnes Daimler omnibus outside Helston Railway Station and with a mixture of fear, excitement and curiosity set off in the direction of England's most southerly point ~ The Lizard. That was the inaugural trip of the Great Western Railway's daily service to open up the peninsula to the rest of the country, the service being advertised upon the timetable in Paddington Station where passengers could buy a ticket that enabled them to complete the entire rail/road journey.

CHAPTER FOUR ~ MEMORIES & FAMILY BUSINESSES

In 1903 the route taken was Helston, Dodson Gap, Cury Cross Lane, Penhale, Ruan Cross Roads and The Lizard. Today, vehicles take in the outlying districts of Poldhu Cove, Mullion, Kugger Crossroad, Ruan Minor, finally arriving in the square at The Lizard.

Various makes of vehicle have been used on the services, the first two being Milnes Daimlers of 16 h.p. These early omnibuses, or cars, as the G.W.R. preferred to call them, were rather

Great Western Railway buses prior to being registered Af36 and Af37 in December 1903 outside Hills Hotel (now the Top House). ~ Mr Jenner is at the wheel on the right ~

photo J. Hart

primitive and breakdowns were very much the order of the day. There were three separate 'change speed' levers, chain drive, oil pumps worked by hand and no windscreens ~ leaving the driver exposed to the elements ~ and solid tyres which cost £200 a set.

In the early years the Helston ~ Lizard service was very much a local service, entire families travelling to and from Helston on Market days, the roof rack fully loaded with crates of chickens and rabbits, baskets of vegetables and fish, and sacks of mail for the Post Office.

After the 1914-18 war expansion of the 'bus' services rapidly spread to other areas. Fierce competition came from the Western National Omnibus Company into which the Great Western Railway services were eventually absorbed in 1933 ~ 30 years after that first 'experimental' trip.

Driving Licence of Harry George Jenner ~
MOTOR CAR ACT, 1903.
LICENCE TO DRIVE MOTOR CAR.

County (Borough) of *Cornwall*.
Harry George Jenner
of *Oliver's Temperance House, Lizard R.S.O.*
is hereby Licensed to drive a Motor Car for the period of twelve months
from the *First* day of *January* 1904
until the *Thirty first* day of *December* 1904
inclusive.
Signed (a) *Christopher L. Coulard*
N.B.—Particulars of any endorsement of any Licence previously held by the person licensed must be entered on the back of this Licence.
IMPORTANT.

Successors to the service maintain a friendly family atmosphere but sadly, the days when the removal of the back seat to accommodate a young calf or pig was commonplace, have long gone!

75 years later, on Sunday 13 August 1978, a cavalcade of vintage vehicles headed by a Western National Omnibus, specially painted by the Company in the livery of the old G.W.R. colours of chocolate and cream with

~ THE LIZARD IN LANDEWEDNACK 113

gold lettering, set off from Helston to re-enact that first historic run. This 'Vintage Car Rally' has now become a popular yearly institution ~ an occasion when the past, just for a brief, while can be relived, attracting as it does, many thousands of veteran car fans and visitors to our Village Green. *Ken Bright*

~ THE SMUGGLERS ~

It is not certain yet where the first Village Post Office was sited ~ there is only a record that Mr Henry Hendy was Sub Postmaster in 1873. However, we know definitely that 'The Smugglers' once did duty as the village Post Office, when in 1893 a Mr Thomas Stirling was the Sub Postmaster. (Many people will remember his son Jackie Stirling).

Shortly after this the Post Office, as we know it today, was built and No. 1 Kynance Terrace then became a Tea Room with rooms to let. Mrs Thomas owned the property which was rented by Mrs Janey Matthews for a number of years.

What is now the Chip Shop part used to be the Chauffeurs' room where the charabanc drivers used to have their meals. The café side used to sell sweets as well and a glass canopy was erected outside where people used to sit to have ice creams.

Prior to the Second World War when the Johnson family were running this restaurant business, water had to be fetched from Rebekkah's Well to fill up a tank in the back yard. This then had to be pumped up to a tank in the loft. American G.I.'s who were billeted there during the war put in the water system upstairs. *Jill and Bob Gubbin.*

~ REBEKKAH'S WELL ~

Rebekkah's Well was named after our Great-grandmother, Rebekkah Stevens, who lived close-by in Pound Cottage. When a child, Rebekkah had attended the local school at a cost of 1d. a week, the school then being on the opposite side of the road to where Landewednack Primary School now stands. Although that first little school has long since been converted into a privately owned bungalow, and prior to 1923 was a carpenter's shop and yard, it is still possible to see the outline of two schoolrooms and a playground! *Francis Triggs*

~ THE POLPEOR CAFÉ ~

The southernmost café in England was built by Mr and Mrs Matthews ~ an old Lizard family ~ in the late 1920s. In those far off summers leading up to the Second World War visitors came for quiet relaxing holidays, and serving as many as 50 customers represented a good day's trading for this small café.

The 1950s and 1960s were Cornwall's 'Golden Years'. Thousands came ~ as they still do ~ to visit The Lizard peninsula. Crab salads prior to and just after the war would have cost an average of 2/11d. (15p). Today they are anything from £5 to £6. A full cream tea then was 2/6d (12^{1}/$_{2}$p) and consisted of two home baked scones, a small dish of strawberry jam, a slice of brown bread and butter, and free choice from a plate of fancy cakes ~ this all served with a pot of tea. Nowadays, 50 years on, a cream tea is usually only a pot of tea with two scones, jam and cream, per person. For this people can expect to pay anything from £2.50 to £3.

In the early 1930s the original owner's daughter, Mrs Winifred Bray, remembers selling her own hand-cranked ice cream at 2d. or 3d. a time ~ her husband going to Newlyn each morning for the ice. The café remained in the Matthews family for over 66 years. Queenie and her husband John ran it themselves for 18 or 19 years. It was then handed over to their son and daughter-in-law, Charles and Nancy. In 1993 the premises were taken over by Peter and Jackie Hendy who have the running of it until the lease expires, when it will pass into the hands of the National Trust. *Winifred Bray*

~ POLPEOR SERPENTINE STONE SHOP ~

The exact date of the construction of this shop is not known but an early photograph of it can be dated around 1880. It was, at that time, the only building on the north side of the car park. Another photograph shows the crew of the *Queen Margaret* resting after having been brought ashore by the lifeboat in 1913. In the background is the shop. Another earlier wreck in 1907 saw part of the cargo from the *S.S.Suevic*, salvaged by local men, auctioned off in the car park by the receivers from Falmouth.

Henry Essex Roberts who was Franklin Roberts' grandfather worked in this shop for most of his life. He originally worked at the Poltesco serpentine factory, and probably moved into the shop when the factory closed down in the mid 1890s. He was one of the very best *turners* and some of the work he did is still available in the village. I purchased the shop in 1976 and hope it will be in our family for many years to come. *P.L.Casley*

~ THE CORNISH STONE SHOP ~

The shop in the Village Square now known as the Cornish Stone Shop was originally two properties dating from 1879. They were sold in 1925 to Mr Cecil Jose and Miss Agnes Roberts for the sum of £9 a piece. Both were serpentine shops and a close inspection will show that the workshop window is still there today. Cecil Jose's grandfather was also the official guide, showing visitors the

Messrs Jose (centre) and Matthews'(right) Serpentine Shops, and Triggs Grocery Shop on The Lizard Green ~

photo F. Triggs

CHAPTER FOUR ~ MEMORIES & FAMILY BUSINESSES

splendid coastline just a walk away from the shop. He was a respected botanist, an authority on the wild flowers which still grow at The Lizard.

Mr Hedley Mundy bought the shops and land over a period of four years between 1928 and 1932. He converted the two shops into one and built the living accommodation above. On his death the property passed to his son, Hedley Granville. In 1988 my mother, Barbara Shipton, and I bought the property which, although improved, still retains today the character of the original two shops. We discovered an old cast iron window which we have made into a feature, and found also newspaper advertising plaques, a reminder of the days when Hedley Mundy Senior sold newspapers. Today we run the family business much as we have always done, but now with the help of my husband, Barry. *Zena Browning*

~ SHEVERA GIFT SHOP ~

The present shop started as a serpentine workshop. In 1933 it was built at a cost of £100 for Mr Wilfred Shipton by Percy Emmett and Leslie Hendy. In 1946 an extension was added, built from secondhand wood purchased from Mr Leonard Casley as building materials were very scarce after the war.

Serpentine continued to be turned until the late 1950s and it was not until 1974 that the lathe shop was converted to a shop window. Mr Shipton continued to run the business until his death in 1969, when Mrs Barbara Shipton took over, soon to be joined by one of her daughters, Zena. The present owners have run the business since they took over in 1988.

Gerald & Sheila Barrett

~ TRINITY COTTAGE ~

Trinity Cottage in Penmenner Road is one of the older properties of The Lizard Village. Until the late 1960s the cottage still had its Cornish range and slate floor. My family (Pascoes) have lived here for four generations. My great-grandparents' children were all born here over 100 years ago, two of them being my grandfather and his sister, who was the great-grandmother of Phil Burgess The Lizard Lifeboat coxswain. It is rumoured that before my family came here the cottage was lived in by lighthouse keepers before the houses were built at the lighthouse ~ hence the name.

Gerald and Sheila Barrett

~ VELVYN'S ~

On approaching the village you will notice, tucked into the lefthand corner of the square, my shop called *Velvyn's*.

Originally it was a potato house owned by Trenoweth Farm, which has recently been altered into self-contained dwellings. The building was once beautifully thatched as is shown in the old postcards. Taken by my grandfather William Roberts and William Shipton it became a serpentine and stone shop. Several of my relatives have worked in the shop ~ among them 'Sweeny' Williams and my late sister Denise Read. I took over the hairdressing business when I was sixteen and remained the village Hair Stylist for some thirty years. I have now changed the salon into a Boutique and Gift Shop.

My late husband, Victor, was a great help to me, both before and after we were married. Over the years he carried out many necessary repairs and always repainted the premises every year. Our son Stuart now helps me with the shop.

Prince George and Princess Mary (later King George V and Queen Mary) came to the village in July 1908 when they bought a piece of serpentine. There was subsequently a board with *patronised by Royalty* placed above the window, and I have had a small plaque made saying *Sponsored by Royalty* which means a great deal to me personally. *Velvyn Burt.*

~ THE NEWSAGENTS AND THE COUNTRY STORE ~

Towards the end of the last century, the Matthews family built a small wooden shop on ground leased from Miss Lyle of Bonython. In the shop serpentine souvenirs were sold. Later sweets, tobacco and newspapers were added to the stock. Sometime after the 1914-18 war a Mr Sanders, who cycled daily from Mullion, rented the property from the Matthews, and turned it into just a tobacconist and newsagents.

The wooden premises were replaced in the early 1930s by a 'bricks and mortar' structure built by Mr Sanders and a Mr Perry ~ a grocer from Helston ~ and comprising two separate shops. Over the years the two shops have changed hands ~ the Newsagents, first to the Step family who ran the business until 1986, when Mr and Mrs J Sherbird took over the lease. In 1996 it was taken over by Jeremy Allerton. The Grocery Store next door was taken over by Mr B. Ives in 1981.

Derry Dobson

~ CORNISH PASTIES ~

The reputation of Cornish Pasties has fluctuated wildly over the years but in this village I have put us firmly on the map with *Ann's Pasties* ~ not only nationally but internationally as well.

It is twelve years since I began to sell my homemade pasties from the small terraced cottage near the village Post Office where I then lived. Today the demand far exceeds supply ~ visitors coming from as far away as Egypt, Singapore and New Zealand to sample one of my pasties.

Ann Muller.

CHAPTER FIVE

New Horizons

~ LIZARD TWINNING ~

The parish of Landewednack is twinned with that of Landevennec in Brittany. The villages share a connection through St Wynwallow (to whom the church in Landewednack is dedicated) who under his Breton name of Guenolé was first abbot of the Benedictine Abbey of Landevennec. No formal connection between the two villages existed however until quite recently.

In 1985 a tentative approach towards twinning was made by Landewednack Parish Council, but not until 1990 was any real contact established. In that year the Bishop of Truro's chaplain led a pilgrimage of six Lizard villagers to the abbey and at a civic function the Mayor of Landevennec expressed an interest in the twinning idea. The following year a second visit by church members to Landevennec and a private visit by the Mayor, M. Roger Lars, to The Lizard, led to further discussion which resulted in a decision by both local councils to support the twinning proposals. In 1992 26 Breton villagers came to Landewednack, and at a dinner firm commitment to twinning was made. On 7 September 1993 the formal twinning Ceremony took place when, after a short service in the Abbey, representatives of both communities met in the Mayor's Parlour in Landevennec. There the Charters were read and signed. At the celebratory dinner which followed gifts were exchanged and friendship cemented.

Since then bi-annual visits by adult members of each community have taken place and in 1995 a party of Lizard Youth Club members travelled to Landevennec where they were entertained by their Breton contemporaries. The Twinning, with its hope for the future, now translates what was once officially described as simply a 'cultural exchange' into a grass roots 'friendship' between the two villages.   *John & Edna Mower*

~ THE WORK OF THE NATIONAL TRUST ~

IN AND AROUND THE LIZARD

The National Trust for Places of Historic Interest and Natural Beauty was founded in 1895 by three social reformers of the day as 'A body of responsible private citizens who would act as trustees for the nation in the acceptance and ownership of land and buildings worthy of permanent preservation'. They saw this as an essential reaction to the growth of population, the spread of industry and residential development, and a lack of planning which was changing the face of England.

A remote area like Cornwall was far from the pressures being felt in southern England and the Lake District, but even here the arrival of the Great Western Railway at Helston in 1887 signalled the beginnings of mass tourism which was to have a profound effect on our landscape, particularly with the development of widespread car ownership after the Second World War.

The founders of the National Trust, like their successors today, were not opposed to development as such but were against unplanned, short-sighted changes which could prove to be to a community's long-term disadvantage. The tension between short and long term points of view is at the heart of many of the sometimes heated debates over the balance of development and conservation in Cornwall. It is easy for the Trust to take a continuing long-term view; equally natural for local people to be conservative about change.

The essence of the Trust as a conservation body is that it works through the ownership and management of land. Moreover it was given by Act of Parliament the power to declare preservation land 'inalienable' i.e. legally incapable of being sold or compulsorily purchased (except by specific parliamentary procedure).

Kynance ~

Although the National Trust had come into possession of coastal land near Tintagel in 1897, it was not until 1935 that a similar acquisition was made at The Lizard. In that year the 'Three Lords' ~ the estates of Tregothnan, Trewithen and Bonython ~in co-operation with the Commons and Open Spaces Society, gave 80 acres of botanically rich heathland running down to Kynance Cove. Even before this, in 1930, the Council for the Preservation of Rural England had commissioned *Cornwall: A survey of its Coast, Moors and Valleys with Suggestions for the Preservation of Amenities* which observed of Kynance Cove:

> *It is considered by the majority to be the most delightful cove on the south coast, and it attracts yearly an immense number of visitors. Formerly the only access was by footpath, but it has been observed that recently the track leading from the Helston ~ Lizard road has been improved and many cars now park on the cliff top above the cove. We suggest that this area ... is eminently worthy of purchase by the National Trust or similar body.*

As increasing numbers of car-borne visitors made their way to Kynance, a house, cafe, shop and stores were developed within the car-park. From there the visitors found their way out onto the Trust's cliff, wearing it away and making it less attractive to others, as well as unwittingly damaging a Site of Special Scientific Interest. By 1974 the situation was serious enough for the government's countryside body, the Countryside Commission, to propose that Kynance should be one of the three key demonstration sites in England where research, consultation and good design could be shown to be the means of reconciling intensive public use with conservation.

In 1986, the car-park development came on the market, and a bequest from Dr Mark Hunter along with money from the Trust's Enterprise Neptune, allowed the purchase of the site and work to begin on making Kynance an easily accessible and pleasant place for up to 250,000 people a year to visit without destroying the delicate and important habitat or reducing the value of the area as an asset to the local tourist economy. With this aim in view the unsatisfactory cliff-staircase was replaced by a gentle path down the valley linking the car-park with the Cove itself.

In 1989 the completed scheme won a Europa Nostra Conservation award and was cited by the British Tourist Authority as a prime example of how tourism and conservation can be reconciled given proper planning and resources. For the Trust the experience served to confirm the importance of its work in supporting local tourist resources, along with the feasibility of restoring damaged landscapes.

Quiet Years and an Awakening ~
In the fifty years between the original acquisition of Kynance and the resolution of its problems, the Trust made two small acquisitions in Landewednack Parish. In 1967 Enterprise Neptune purchased $3^{1}/_{2}$ acres of cliff at Bass Point, including the freehold of the then operational Coastguard Lookout and the adjoining day mark. In 1976 followed 27 acres of Parn Voose Cove north of Church Cove, with the long abandoned quarry. Funding came from a variety of sources, including the Caravan Club of Great Britain.

Real progress at The Lizard was prompted by two events. In 1981 Mr Cyril Medley of Budliegh Salterton left a substantial legacy for the purchase of 'unspoilt coastal land' in the southern part of The Lizard. Then in 1987 Miss Robina Wallis bequeathed to the trust, Wartha Manor, her substantial but dilapidated 1890s Victorian house overlooking Lizard Point, along with five acres of land. The bequest was conditional on the offer being accepted within six months and on the property being declared inalienable. Inalienability is reserved for property of national importance and, although interesting, Wartha Manor cannot claim national distinction in itself. However, the circumstances spurred the Trust to explore the possibility of acquiring the adjoining land lying between Lizard Head and the Most Southerly Point. This proved possible due to the co-operation of the vendors and to Mr Medley's legacy. So Wartha Manor became an integral part of a coastal landscape of inalienable quality. All this was celebrated by a tea party at the house where the guest of honour, author and critic, J.C. Trewin, described his childhood memories of the area in the years of the First World War, as recorded in his book *Up from The Lizard*.

Wartha Manor though, still posed two problems for the Trust. The building was in a dilapidated state and there was an unexpected expense connected with the estate which had to be met. This latter was solved by a hitherto unknown treasure trove of elegant designer dresses and shoes from the 1930s found hidden away in trunks and cupboards, which sold well at auction in London. The repair of the house was secured by restoring the house to its original state.

Seeing the Point ~
The Trust now found itself an immediate neighbour to the Most Southerly Point, a site as significant as Land's End and, with Kynance Cove, the principal asset of the local tourist economy. However visitors' enjoyment was marred by severe traffic congestion and consequent danger to pedestrians on the narrow lane from Lizard Green to the Point. Following the death of Mr Robert Lyle in 1991, the Bonython Estate sold the Point to the Trust with much of the land lying between it and the village; again, the purchase was made possible by Mr Medley's bequest. A much needed path for pedestrians was built alongside the

road, separated from it by half a mile of new Cornish hedge built with carefully selected stone to match the local geology. Grant aid from a number of sources allowed one and threequarter miles of overhead electricity and telephone wires to be put underground, restoring some of the landscape's original character. Further land purchases enabled the path to be extended from the Lighthouse car-park through to the Point itself and the demolition of some derelict buildings with the provision of modern toilet facilities discreetly sited.

Whole Landscape Approach ~

Ownership of the Point and close working with the Parish, District and County Councils to resolve some of the long-standing problems, drew the Trust into looking overall at The Lizard Point landscape, defined as the land lying south of the village between Lizard Head in the west and Bass Point in the east. Apart from the beauty of the coast and the Most Southerly Point's special sense of place, equally important is the botanical richness of the unfarmed cliffs, a Grade 1* Site of Special Scientific Interest and a proposed Special Area of Conservation, the highest level of native conservation designation in Europe. Equally the land is an important source of employment, both in terms of farming and the tourist industry.

In 1992 the Trust bought the ageing Polbream Hotel from the receiver, because of its integral relationship with The Lizard Lighthouse complex, itself to be sold following automation in 1997. the idea would be for the Lighthouse's character to remain unchanged with the redundant accommodation to be put to uses of benefit to the local community and economy.

Lloyd's Signal Station served as a key source of communication with the busy shipping channels of the Western Approaches from 1872 until 1950 when it became a private house. By 1993 when it came on the market again little of its historical character remained, either internally or externally. Thanks to a bequest the Trust was able to buy it through Enterprise Neptune, while the sale of a long lease and grants provided for its restoration.

In 1994 Tregullas Farm and most of the land not already owned by the Trust between Lizard Head and Bass Point became available, and was bought by the Trust. The farm had been intensively farmed with a dairy herd and root crops. Its purchase gave the opportunity to review the enterprises and land use in the context of the overall landscape. The scientific importance of the cliffs will certainly benefit from the adjoining coastal fields being managed less intensively as semi-natural grassland, whilst in the long-term creating a habitat in their own right and a sympathetic landscape blend. The farm has been relet to a local farmer, and the traditional farm buildings are being restored and adapted for new productive uses.

It is hoped that by the year 2000 all current projects will have been completed and the resulting enrichment of the landscape for visitors and local people alike will be seen as a permanent public benefit, very much in the spirit of the Trust's founders a hundred years ago.

This large programme of works has been made possible by grants from the European Regional Development Fund, Countryside Commission, Rural Development Commission and local Councils. *Peter Mansfield*

Kynance Cove

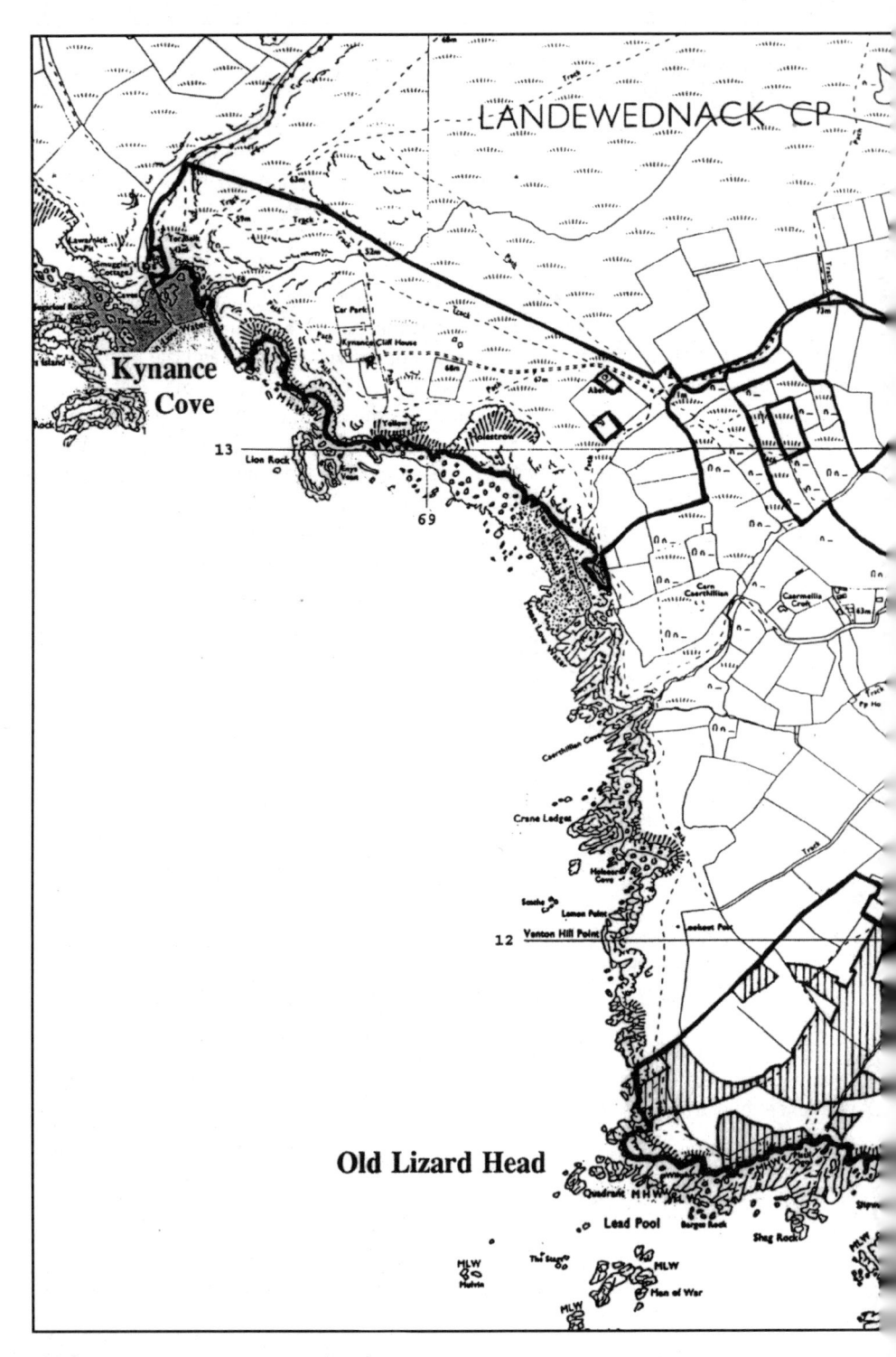

13 Lion Rock

69

12 Venton Hill Point

Old Lizard Head

Lead Pool

LEGEND

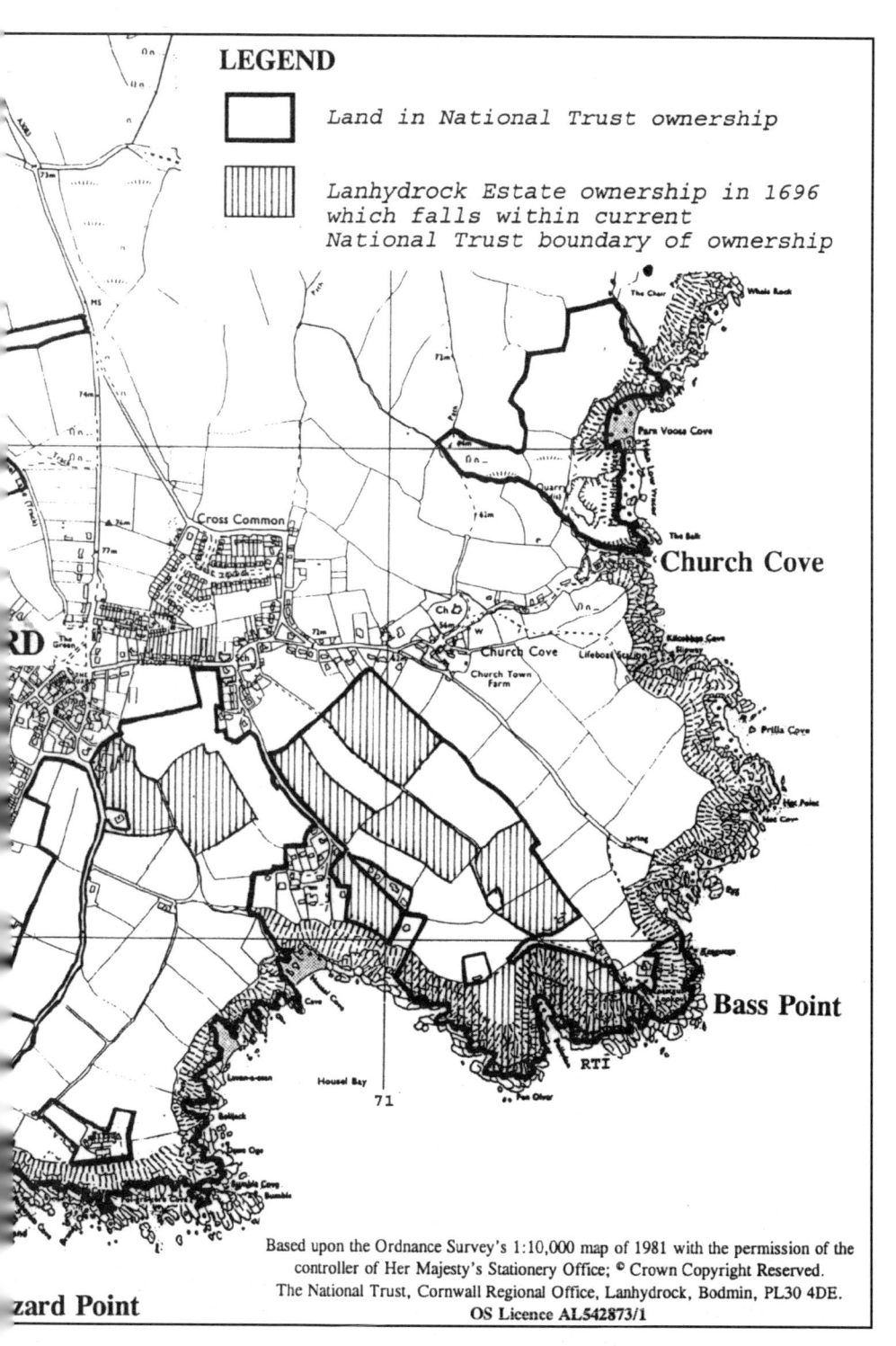

▢ Land in National Trust ownership

▦ Lanhydrock Estate ownership in 1696 which falls within current National Trust boundary of ownership

Church Cove

Bass Point

Based upon the Ordnance Survey's 1:10,000 map of 1981 with the permission of the controller of Her Majesty's Stationery Office; © Crown Copyright Reserved. The National Trust, Cornwall Regional Office, Lanhydrock, Bodmin, PL30 4DE.
OS Licence AL542873/1

ACKNOWLEDGMENTS

The Lizard History Society would like to thank all those who have contributed in any way to the making of this book. Special thanks go to Eileen Gamble for preparing the cover designs; William Hocking for his photographic work; Andre Ellis for his original drawings and map; to June Palmer for her advice, and to Dave Lewis for his valuable assistance. To the Cornwall County Record Office, the Cornish Studies Library, Trinity House, Landewednack Parish Council and the late F.S. Dunn we record our thanks for their help with research; and to the National Trust for their interest and practical support. Last but not least, thanks go to the Leader Project for making publication possible.

ILLUSTRATIONS : ~
PHOTOGRAPHS LOANED BY:~

W. Hocking	Pages 12/39/44/80/95
J. Hart	Pages Back Cover/13/18/29/30/37/56 57/85/92/97/113
F.E. Gibson	Page Front Cover
Helston Museum	Page 9
A. Stiles	Page 15
E. Hart	Page 33
P. Mitchell	Page 71
F. Triggs	Page 115

DRAWINGS BY:~

A. Ellis	Pages 2-3/16/21/41/48
Unknown	Page 23

'The Most Southerly Post Office' p57. Attempts to contact the copyright holder of 'Through the Letter Box, 1988', from which this extract has been taken, have proved unsuccessful.

Easily available books about Landewednack which you might like to read:
C.A Johns ~ A WEEK AT THE LIZARD, 1848 ~ Reprinted by Llanrech Press 1992
D.M. Craik ~ AN UNSENTIMENTAL JOURNEY, 1884 ~ Reprinted by the Jamieson Library 1988
J.C Trewin ~ UP FROM THE LIZARD, 1948 ~ Carroll and Nicholson
W. Best Harris ~ THE LIZARD COASTLINE ~ privately printed, no date
J. Lawman ~ NATURAL HISTORY OF THE LIZARD PENINSULA 1994 ~ Institute of Cornish Studies.

NOTES ~

NOTES ~